This book provided by

Reverend Leo J. Tibesar

Pastor of St. Frances Cabrini Church
1994-2011

Judaism
Does Not Equal
Israel

Also by Marc H. Ellis

Toward a Jewish Theology of Liberation

Out of the Ashes:
The Search for Jewish Identity
in the Twenty-first Century

Reading the Torah Out Loud:
A Journey of Lament and Hope

Judaism
Does Not Equal
Israel

Marc H. Ellis

THE NEW PRESS

NEW YORK
LONDON

Requests for permission to reproduce selections from this book should be mailed to: Permissions Department, The New Press, 38 Greene Street, New York, NY 10013.

Published in the United States by The New Press, New York, 2009
Distributed by Perseus Distribution

LIBRARY OF CONGRESS CATALOGING-IN-PUBLICATION DATA

Ellis, Marc H.
Judaism does not equal Israel :
Marc H. Ellis.
p. cm.
Includes bibliographical references.
ISBN 978-1-59558-425-0 (hc. : alk. paper)   1. Israel and the diaspora.
2. Jews—United States—Attitudes toward Israel.
3. Jews—Identity.   4. Arab-Israeli conflict.
5. Holocaust (Jewish theology)   6. Prophets.
7. Israel—Ethnic relations.   I. Title.
DS132.E56 2009
305.892'4—dc22 2008042165

The New Press was established in 1990 as a not-for-profit alternative to the large, commercial publishing houses currently dominating the book publishing industry. The New Press operates in the public interest rather than for private gain, and is committed to publishing, in innovative ways, works of educational, cultural, and community value that are often deemed insufficiently profitable.

www.thenewpress.com

Composition by dix!
This book was set in New Caledonia
Map on p. xxiii by Justin K. Waters

Printed in the United States of America

2   4   6   8   10   9   7   5   3   1

Contents

Foreword by Archbishop Desmond Tutu   vii

Preface   ix

1. At the Crossroads of Jewish Identity   1

    A Godless Judaism?   11

    Searching for My *Other* Voice   29

    In the Homes of Martyrs   44

2. The Jewish Quest for Liberation   53

    The Outer Limits of Jewish Dissent   62

    Confronting the Holocaust and State Zionism   74

    Israel Burning   95

3. Can Jews Redeem Christianity?   102

    The Failure of the Ecumenical Dialogue   116

    Christian Holocaust Theology   124

    Divesting Apartheid   132

4. Mapping Jewish Destiny   149

    The Boundaries of Jewish Destiny   155

    Confessing in the Presence of the Burning Children   165

    A Wounding Ambivalence   179

5. Prophets in Exile   194

   Un-Jewish   195

   The Mezuzah on Our Doorpost   205

   The Prophetic Wild Card   208

Epilogue: Mourning for the Future   212

Notes   226

Foreword

Archbishop Desmond Tutu

I thank God for my Hebrew antecedents and their Bible. Our New Testament is incomprehensible without its Jewish roots. When apartheid's repression was at its most vicious, this tradition and its great prophets inspired us and sustained our hope in the ultimate triumph of good over evil, of freedom over injustice and oppression, of peace over violence and hatred. They taught us that God is notoriously biased, forever taking the side of the weak, the oppressed, the downtrodden against the kings and the powerful elite.

All of the Hebrew scriptures depict a just and merciful God, and if God's people would be holy, they must perform mundane acts of caring, of kindness, of compassion, and of humanitarian concern. In Deuteronomy the clear motive for kindness to the widow, the orphan, and the alien is not just holiness, it is the memory of slavery in Egypt. That memory should prevent their inflicting on others the same anguish.

Jews are indispensable for a just and caring world. We need Jews faithful to their scriptures and to their prophetic vocation; these have meant so much for the world's morality—

for our sense of what sets oppressed people free and of what is just.

Equating the state of Israel with Judaism threatens with irrelevance the prophetic power and truth of the scriptures that have, for millennia, inspired and grounded Jews in their witness to God. Israel's treatment of the Palestinian people reminds me of Cape Town under apartheid: coloreds thrown out of their homes and relocated in distant ghetto townships, illegal walls encroaching on people's ancient lands, separated families, divided properties, and the nightmare of running military checkpoint gauntlets.

I thank God for Marc Ellis, a faithful Jew who is committed to renewing prophetic Judaism. Jews may reject their religious calling and survive for a long time, but equating the nation-state of Israel and its military might with prophetic Judaism will corrode both from the inside out. Upholding an unjust collusion of religion with a militaristic state corrodes a people's humanity. Ellis's work is important not only to the survival of Judaism as a religious tradition but also to untangling what has been the terrible political tragedy of Israel's policies against the Palestinians.

Marc Ellis calls upon Jews to hear again the cry of the oppressed in their midst, see their anguish, and follow a God who delivers the downtrodden. He calls them to remember Egypt and Germany and to deal with the oppressed, the weak, and the despised compassionately and caringly. He speaks from the depth of his heart, to all his spiritual relatives. Please, please hear the noble call of our scriptures to do justice, love mercy, and walk humbly with God.

Preface

The prophetic is the wild card of Jewish life and its primordial marker. Jewish life cannot be described without the prophetic, which always pushes Judaism to another dimension. In these pages I hold the prophetic marker of Judaism against its corrupting—and potentially fatal—identification with modern Israel. I also offer a prophetic, life-giving way forward for Jewish life in the world.

Like life itself, the journey through Jewish life is rarely linear. It is the negotiation of a maze with diverted paths, hidden clues, and few good maps. To forge a clear path forward is hard work. It demands exploration on personal, communal, and historical levels. In Jewish life, both individuality and community count. So do history, the prophetic, and God.

The great twentieth-century Jewish theologian Martin Buber referred to the prophetic as the indigenous sign of the people called Israel. He found the prophetic in the origins of the biblical Israel and believed that this ancient moral force journeys with the people Israel forever. If we follow Buber's understanding to its logical conclusion, explanations of Jewish life become difficult, if not impossible, without it.

In every generation Jews seek and establish an "orderly" life that will inevitably be undermined. It may even be undermined in the very generation that has established or reestablished an orderly way of being Jewish. Think of the recent history central to contemporary Jewish identity. In the twentieth century Jews underwent a thorough modernization and secularization, survived the Holocaust, and experienced a demographic shift unparalleled in Jewish history—the population center of Jews shifted from Europe to North America and Israel—and gained economic, social, and political power in the United States.

The current map of Jewish life has changed so considerably that its continuity and discontinuity with the past are debated endlessly. Is Jewish life in the twenty-first century continuous with the Jewish history that has gone before us? Or are Jews embarking on a path so different as to require a radical makeover of the term "Jewish"?

Jewish identity is internal to our communal life, like every other religious tradition. At the same time, no community is an island. As a distinct minority people for much of our history, Jews have developed internal mechanisms for adjusting to the external demands made on us. The twentieth century, especially, made radical demands on us and elicited a vastly changed map of Jewish life.

The Holocaust and its aftermath were the external world's profound intrusion on the internal workings of Jewish life. With their genocidal agenda, the Nazis irrevocably changed internal Jewish identity. The Nazis forced a recon-

sideration of the trajectory of Jewish life and the require-
ments to meet its new course.

The Jewish state of Israel, created just three years after
the Holocaust, in 1948, is the main exemplar of that new
course. The political and state power mobilized in the wake
of the Holocaust are unprecedented in the previous two
thousand years of Jewish life. This new course thoroughly re-
oriented Jewish life; the ways Jews practiced politics and religion all underwent revision in light of the establishment of
Israel. This change has been so massive that some Jewish
scholars, myself included, wonder if Judaism should now be
referred to as post-Holocaust Judaism or post-Holocaust
Jewish life.

Post-Holocaust Judaism has become the religion Jews
affirm that most Jews have little to do with. A majority of
Jews today have very little in their lives of ritual or rules. For
far more Jews, self-identification with Israel is more important than religious observance. The Israel in question is the
modern state of Israel, rather than the people Israel. That
this Israel is clearly more important to Jews than Judaism is
unsurprising to contemporary observers of Jewish life.

This equation of Jewish identity with the nation Israel is
a thoroughly modern one. The history of Judaism stretches
more than five thousand years, but the modern state of Israel
has just reached its sixtieth year. For most of our history, Jews
have been without a state of our own. Should we then con-
flate Jewish identity with this modern Israel?

Judaism today is, in fact, not simply to be equated with

the state of Israel. Jewish life encompasses a variety of paths.
It includes prophetic Judaism, the memory of the Holocaust,
cultural and spiritual understandings of Zionism, forms of
Jewish renewal, and the state of Israel. So "Jewish" includes
certain religious understandings and practices, as well as diverse perspectives on Jewish history and identity.

Minority factions seek to define what Jewish means
within the ever-evolving maze of Jewish life. These factions
include Jewish leaders with the means and status to exert
their vision within and beyond the Jewish community. Also,
however, there is a burgeoning number of Jews who oppose
Judaism's equation with the nation Israel. This latter group
has been cast into exile from mainstream Jewish life.

The current Jewish establishment seeks a religion-state
alliance, parallel to that which early Christianity forged with
the imperial state, an alliance also sought by the current
Christian religious Right in the United States. This alliance is
often called Constantinian Christianity, and it is mirrored by
a Constantinian Judaism. The dissenters from this establishment Jewish identity I call "Jews of Conscience." Jews of
Conscience experience Jewish life as imbued with questions
of justice. Constantinian Jews are defined by their pursuit
and exercise of power, Jews of Conscience by their pursuit of
ethics and exercise of conscience. Both seek the best for Jews
and the Jewish community. They see Judaism and the path to
pursue it from very different perspectives.

The stakes in this struggle to define Judaism and Jewish
life are the highest possible. Hence, Constantinian Jews and
Jews of Conscience battle over the means to achieve the ends

they pursue. This battle is an ongoing civil war. A third group, progressive Jews, stands midway between Constantinian Jews and Jews of Conscience. These Jews seek to negotiate between the other two groups, but in the end, they are closer to the first than to the second. Progressive Jews embody the paradox that we often become like those we seek to displace as we try to overpower them. Progressive equations of order attempt to balance the human need for stability with the concomitant human need for freedom and diversity. The order equation tends, however, to subsume these needs within its own orbit. Equations seek balance; they are an act or process of making things stable, not equal. Too often, order is the heavy hand of power disguised as peacemaking.

Seeking balance is more comforting in the short run, and facile equations make things easily defined and balanced. Deeper readings of both sides of an equation can challenge stabilities and their seemingly smooth path to the future. When we do this deeper analysis, the progressive equation takes on more troubling and dissonant dimensions. Thoughtful analyses of power untangle the progressive equation and expose the variables that form the equation and their inherent inequalities.

Deeper readings upset what we think we know. They disturb the boundaries set forth by those who have the knowledge, wealth, and status to define and control Judaism. They challenge us to find a new way forward. They demand thought and compassion. Conscience requires us to seek a world beyond the boundaries set forth, to draw different boundaries that redefine the individual and the community.

This disturbing of the boundaries opens dangerous territory. Since boundaries are important for our individual and collective lives, they must be examined with care. Still, if current boundaries are found wanting, we have a responsibility to search out new boundaries for individual and collective identity. The fences of Holocaust-defined Judaism and Jewish life have obscured another reality that has profound internal consequences for a Jewish future and any religious claims that can be identified as Judaism.

Coterminous with the Holocaust and the founding of Israel have been the conquest and destruction of much of Palestine. The creation of Israel forced an ethnic cleansing of more than seven hundred thousand Palestinians to create room for the Jewish state. The removal of Palestinians from their own land continued through the early years of Israel's existence. It accelerated in the wake of the 1967 Arab-Israeli war. These policies continue today in the Jewish "settlements"—really expansive towns and small cities—that mark the future of Israel's dominant and permanent presence in Jerusalem and the West Bank.

"Ethnic cleansing" has been protested and mourned in Jewish identity as something that happens *to* Jews. That Jews used ethnic cleansing to form the state of Israel introduces another, profoundly disturbing factor in the formation of modern Jewish identity. It appears our empowerment is tainted with the same abuse of power others have used against us, an abuse we have condemned. To admit this equation— "What has been done to us we have done to others"—is to acknowledge that we have become like those we condemn.

The indigenous marker of Judaism, the prophetic, was originally used to condemn the Egyptians when we were slaves. It was later turned inward to judge the people Israel when we attained power within the Land. Jewish institutions and identity based in modern Israel have pointed the accusing finger only at others. The prophetic binary dynamic may finally be reasserting itself, however, in the post-Holocaust period. Some of us suggest we should also be pointing the prophetic finger at ourselves.

What, then, are the consequences of this realization? On the one hand, it might mean the need to abandon our empowerment in the state of Israel. This would necessitate a reappraisal of the power we wield in America. On the other hand, it might require only a reevaluation of the way we use that power, an ethical modification. If either course is followed, the consequences for Jewish identity in the twenty-first century will be profound.

What if part or even the majority of the Jewish community refuses this reevaluation of Israel? For those beyond the borders of the majority Jewish community, we must seek to discover what we can affirm as "authentically" Jewish. Being a minority has long defined Jews and Judaism. American Jews make up a small minority of the American population. Jews are still a distinct minority within the world, and Israel is a small state within a much larger international nation-state system. Israel as a Jewish state is increasingly isolated in the international community. Hence, any redefinition of what it means to be Jewish will affect the Jewish future. Should dissenting Jews in the minority continue to struggle within the community for a new definition of what it means to be Jewish? Or, having struggled and lost, must we leave the community, claiming another definition of what it means to be Jewish?

Jewish life has settled into a self-understanding that revolves around the Holocaust; Jewish assertions of power are seen as a response to this fundamental injustice. Hence the axiomatic equation of Jewish life: "Jewish power equals innocence." Another way of stating that equation is "Israel equals innocence." Or "Jews and Israel equal innocence." Their corollary is: "Those who doubt Jewish and Israeli innocence are anti-Semitic." This corollary asserts that those who challenge the formation of Israel and the linking of Jewish identity with it must be against Jewish identity itself.

This corollary assumes that all critiques of Israel harbor the same anti-Semitic sentiments as those from the past. The charge of anti-Semitism is even leveled against those Jews who dissent from the "Jewish power equals innocence" identity formulation. We are labeled "self-hating" Jews, Jews who doubt Israel's innocence and have such difficulty with a positive Jewish identity that we desire to make our fellow Jews subservient to non-Jews. Accusations of anti-Semitism and Jewish self-hatred are the flip side of the counterfeit claim that Jewish power is innocent.

All communities have contested identities. Few communities have so much at stake as Jewish communities. Much blood has been shed over the "Jewish question," as it has been known over the millennia. What is in contention is no less than what it means to be Jewish and, in the cauldron of power politics, what it takes for Jews to survive and flourish in an uncertain and dangerous world. This contested identity has become the focal point of the civil war within the Jewish world. We think of warfare as coming primarily from outside the Jewish community, but, in fact, internal strife has often erupted over what it means to be Jewish. The future may have more of the same in store. The outcome of this civil war will largely determine what "Jewish" means for Jews themselves and the world at large.

The Bible tells the story of a people enslaved in Egypt and that people's struggle for freedom as the central drama of Jewish history. At the center of that drama is the one and true God. Could there be a narrative of liberation more powerful than the one told in the Hebrew Bible? It is the bedrock of the prophetic, the moral voice of protest against abuses of power.

In these pages I explore the Jewish narrative as it has come to be in the twenty-first century, its allies, and its implications for the future. In doing so, I highlight its contested claims and point to a future worth bequeathing to our children.

As a Jew, I do not pretend to be a disinterested observer. As for all Jews, the stakes for me are high. Though I am enfolded in Jewish history and rest content within that fold, I have a responsibility to see a way forward and state that way as an option for my own people.

In chapter 1 I describe my struggle to articulate my dissent. Especially when he or she is critical of the directions of the Jewish community, every Jew must find his or her own voice. Much is at stake in finding that voice, and raising it is even more difficult. My childhood and early adult years paralleled many of the post-Holocaust developments that have shaped contemporary Jewish identity. Studying the Holocaust in the early 1970s, while it was being named and shaped, allowed me a window into the discussions and debates that followed as the Holocaust became central to Jewish identity. So, too, I lived through the 1967 Arab-Israeli war, which saw Israel become central to Jewish identity. I follow this emerging centrality and the questions that come from the attitudes and policies that followed, especially regarding the plight of the Palestinian people and accusations of the "new" anti-Semitism applied to them and their supporters in the world.

As I experienced the Holocaust and Israel becoming central to Jewish identity, I also came to know the Palestinians on a personal level. Starting in 1973 and increasingly after 1984, I visited Palestinians in their homes in Jerusalem, the West Bank, and Gaza. These visits became more and more formative for my life as a post-Holocaust Jew. My journey among Palestinians made me realize that my generation of Jews came *after* the Holocaust and *after* Israel.

This journey after the Holocaust and Israel led me to construct a Jewish theology of liberation. Chapter 2 is a reflection on how I began to piece together my dissenting voice in this theology. I trace my being at the origins of what came to be known as Holocaust theology—that is, consciousness of the Holocaust. It was written by Jews interested in the meaning of the Holocaust for Jewish life and a Jewish future, as well as in the almost simultaneous struggle to define the meaning of the Holocaust in a broader way. I challenge the Jewish post-Holocaust identity that sees only uncritical support for Israel as the norm. I ask, if only Israel is important, how can we see our broader responsibilities for others? A narrow view of Jewish support for Israel may not even be good for Israel in the long run. A Jewish theology of liberation raises the question of how a suffering Jewish people should proceed ethically, once we attain power. Does power itself liberate? Can power offer liberation from suffering if another people, in this case the Palestinians, is suffering so that Jews can have power? I describe how I found different ways of looking at the lessons of the Holocaust and alternative ways of understanding the creation of Israel.

Chapter 3 moves into the Christian community after the Holocaust. As an oppressive presence in Jewish life, Christian anti-Semitism laid the groundwork for Nazi-inspired genocide and was historically culpable in the Holocaust. In parallel with Jewish Holocaust theology, a new understanding of Christianity emerged. This Christian understanding romanticized Jews, a reversal of Christian tradition, which demonized Jews. Much of this renewed Christianity took place in an ecumenical Jewish-Christian dialogue that emerged after the Holocaust. This dialogue took on momentum after Israel's victory in the 1967 war. The Jewish partners in the dialogue concentrated on the need for Christianity to rid itself of the scourge of anti-Semitism and demanded uncritical loyalty to Israel as a sign of Christian repentance for Christians' sins against the Jewish people.

From the Jewish vantage point, criticism of Israel meant a renewed anti-Semitism; thus, the ecumenical dialogue morphed into what I call the "ecumenical deal." This ecumenical deal became a political deal in which, at least in the American political system, any politician who criticized Israel was smeared and quickly dispatched into private life. Having witnessed aspects of the ecumenical and political deal, I ask whether this deal is good for Christians or for Jews, whether this demonstrates a real friendship and solidarity with Jews or cowardice. In order to move forward as Jews and Christians do we need to break the ecumenical deal?

In chapter 4 I try to understand the concrete situation in Israel and Palestine. Maps allow us to see the facts on the ground. Using the maps from the Wye River Conference between Israelis and Palestinians in 1998 as a point of reference, I trace the reality of Israel's expansion, Palestine's diminishment, and the Palestinian remnant populations created since the founding of Israel. By referencing maps before and after this conference, we can see the permanence of the Israeli occupation in Jerusalem and the West Bank. Jews also need to look at the map of 1948, when Israel was created and the majority of Palestinians living in the Land were driven out of what became Israel. The Wye River Conference gives us a window into the never-ending peace process and what it actually achieves. Then we can ask the question of where we want to move from these facts and what might help us to move beyond the rhetoric on all sides of a civil war within the Jewish community. How do these maps comport with the map of the Holocaust, and what is to be done with these maps of Jewish life? Do these maps point toward a healing of the trauma of the Holocaust or a deepening of that trauma? If these maps are the maps of Jewish destiny, where will they take us?

Chapter 5 explores the reemergence of the Jewish prophetic voice in our time. Jewish life has a history of prophetic figures arising within the Jewish community. In ancient times, the community claimed that the prophets were outside the Judaic framework and needed to be censored. Often they were handed over to non-Jewish authorities, or the Jewish establishment itself took care of them. Sadly, this is no different today; Jews who claim that only Jewish power can protect Jews from another Holocaust regularly hand over Jews of Conscience. However, like the ancient biblical prophets, Jews of Conscience are the wild card of the Jewish future. Just when power seems to have packaged everything in imperial wrapping—so that the future is beholden to and responsible for the empire—the prophet unravels this unjust path by demanding justice and moral community.

Jews of Conscience on the margins of the Jewish world are preparing for a Jewish future beyond injustice and empire. Jews, having given the prophetic to the world, have always been ambivalent about that very same prophetic. Important Jewish thinkers point toward and away from the prophetic. Regardless of all attempts to expel, explain away, or eliminate it, the prophetic remains. It is the wild card of Jewish life.

These pages conclude with a lament and a plea. Judaism is now aligned with power. In its abuses of power, Jewish life has already been altered beyond imagining. This, I lament. If Jewish life is to continue, it will have to be reformed. Can it disentangle itself from imperial power and still survive?

Judaism does not equal Israel.

If Judaism disentangles itself from Israel, can Israel survive that disentanglement? Judaism and Israel may be on the brink of dissolution. Could that also represent the beginning of a new Jewish way after the Holocaust and Israel?

The end is always near. What matters is the beginning that comes after. I will not experience what comes after, even though it has begun in my lifetime. Coming from the post-Holocaust generation, I am, like others, formed by the times in which I live. It is up to the next generation to form its own equations—and to undo those that have come before it. Though I will not fully experience the new life to come, I can sense that newness in my own lament and a new generation that laments with me.

After the landscape of destruction and death that was created for us in Europe and after the destruction and death we have now visited upon others in Israel/Palestine, even a taste of this newness is a blessing. Blessings take on a deeper meaning after a long struggle endured along the way.

Gratitude is essential to life. Can we be grateful for the struggle to be faithful?

We are always on our way. So it was. So it is. So it will be. Being on our way, we must be for others. How else can we also be for ourselves?

Wye Memorandum, 1998

0 ____ 20 km

Jenin

Tulkarm

Qalqilya

Nablus

ARIEL

UPPER
MODI'IN

Ramallah

GIV'AT
ZE'EV

Jericho

ISRAEL

Jerusalem

MA'ALE
ADUMIM

BETAR

Bethlehem

Green Line

Dead Sea

Hebron

■ Palestinian Autonomous Areas
(Oslo II-Zones A and B)

□ Projected areas of further
Israeli redeployment

▨ Israeli settlement,
projected extent

▧ Designated nature reserve

▲ Israeli settlement

**Palestinian Academic Society for the
Study of International Affairs
(PASSIA)**

Map discussed in Chapter 4

At the Crossroads of Jewish Identity

On the centenary of the great Jewish theologian Abraham Joshua Heschel, I hosted a celebration at my university, a Baptist institution in central Texas. Heschel's daughter Susannah keynoted the event. An important Jewish scholar in her own right, she is also guardian of her father's great legacy. With her were a number of younger Jewish scholars from all over the country, Europe, and Israel—three generations of Jews meeting and discussing what had been, what is, and what might become the future.

Abraham Joshua Heschel was born at the turn of the twentieth century, the scion of a prominent Hasidic family in Poland. Fleeing Nazi Europe, he arrived in the United States in 1940 where he became perhaps the most prominent Jewish theologian of the century. Most of his family did not escape the Nazis; his mother and three sisters died in the Holocaust.

Heschel was a rabbi, scholar, and prophet. His university training in Berlin began his journey into the heart of European Christianity and modernity. He continued his family's heritage in his newfound home, and developed his modern sensibilities. Because of the Holocaust and the changing world for Jews and non-Jews alike, Heschel spent the second half of his life in the challenging, disorienting, and fruitful Diaspora.[1]

I knew of Heschel through his works and met him once as a university student just months before he died in 1972. Though my meeting with him was brief, it was intense, so intense that I recall it easily today. After his main lecture, a reception for Heschel was held in the small Christian chapel on campus. With a few faculty and students, I sat with Heschel—literally at his feet, as he sat on a chair. I was twenty years old; he was sixty-five, my grandfather's age. Heschel looked weary.

Heschel was from another world, and like my grandparents, European born. They arrived in America ahead of Heschel, in the early 1900s. My grandparents knew and spoke Yiddish to each other, though by the time I knew them, they spoke English without an accent. Heschel had a decided accent. That and his Jewish learning marked him as an Eastern European Jewish sage, and his travels through America must have presented to him an entirely different world. This difference applied to the American Jewish world as well. Though Heschel became known and influential, he would never quite fit into his adopted Jewish community. Until his death he was an outsider looking in; he rarely liked what he saw in contemporary American Jewish life.

I knew this difficulty firsthand. My university teacher, Richard Rubenstein, had been a rabbinical student of Heschel's. In 1966 Rubenstein published an explosive book, *After Auschwitz: Radical Theology and Contemporary Judaism*. In it, Rubenstein broke with Heschel's embrace of a

God of history. What could Jews say about this God *after* Auschwitz?[2]

This *after* was troubling to Heschel and to other Jews. In years to come, Rubenstein's question challenged Jewish and Christian understandings of what could and could not be said about God. If God is the God of the covenant, promising to be with the people Israel through history, where was God during the Holocaust?

Heschel asserted emphatically that God was an active presence in the world after the Holocaust, and he spent the 1950s and early 1960s lecturing American Jews on precisely this issue. In those years, the Holocaust had yet to become the main orientation of the Jewish world; perhaps it was too near and explosive to be touched. Instead, science and psychology had struck at the core of the Jewish belief in an ancient and distinct God. In much of the Jewish community, Jewish identity and communal belonging were being argued without placing God at the center.

The argument that God and the Jewish liturgy were symbolic infuriated Heschel. A dynamic and courageous person, he chastised Jewish leaders for leading Jews into a world stripped of their distinctiveness and calling. Jews without God, the real God of Israel, were something other than Jews. But how could Jewish leaders direct Jews back to God if they had already given up on that reality?

People lined up on both sides of Heschel's defense of God. His challenge to both sides was not limited, however, to the question of God's existence. Heschel's God led to social justice. This consciousness of justice was grounded in his sojourn in Europe, where Jews were deprived of rights and life. His consciousness developed in America beginning in the 1950s, as Heschel perceived civil rights as a fundamental test of America's political and religious fiber. Later he protested against the Vietnam War. In both movements, Heschel joined forces with ecumenical and interfaith leaders, such as Martin Luther King Jr., who directly challenged American racism and foreign policy.

Heschel stirred controversy on a variety of fronts while also encouraging Jewish religious and justice-oriented action. On the God front, Heschel laid the responsibility for Auschwitz at the hands of a humanity devoid of God. Human responsibility, rather than the absence of God, was at fault. To the question of why God did not intervene to stop the slaughter, Heschel was without an answer. The best he could do was appeal to an ancient Jewish tradition of God hiding his face. Humanity was responsible; God was unavailable.

This hidden dimension, for Heschel, deepened the mystery of God. Regardless of how one wrestled with the question of God, the abandonment of belief in God signaled disaster. Without a real God that we could search for and a God that could search for us, Heschel thought, humanity would be left bereft of meaning and possibility. If God was not real and tangible, all religions, Judaism included, were shams.

Heschel swam against the current of American Judaism as it was evolving in the 1950s and 1960s—America *was* different from Europe, and American Jews were different from those in Europe. He also swam against an even stronger current of Holocaust consciousness that was consolidating in the wake of the 1967 Arab-Israeli war. Only after Israel's victory against its Arab neighbors did Holocaust consciousness grow in America. The merging of Jewish power and Jewish suffering became a tidal wave engulfing Jewish institutions, Jewish philanthropy, and Jewish intellectual life. Could such a tidal wave spare Jewish theology?

Jews of my generation lived at the intersection of Heschel's radicalism and Rubenstein's questioning of God. As a Jew born in the 1950s and coming of age in the 1960s, I felt the call of the Jewish commitment to justice. John F. Kennedy and Martin Luther King Jr. were heroes in my home and in my life. At the same time, Rubenstein's questions about God and humanity after Auschwitz affected me deeply.

For a long time, I took what I could from both Heschel and Rubenstein, but I could not fully embrace either Heschel's God or Rubenstein's pessimism. Rubenstein's pessimism moved toward a neoconservatism that later engulfed the Jewish community. That same neoconservatism ultimately reaffirmed God, or at least some notion of God. Certainly a strong Jewish identity emerged; its backdrop was a world that neoconservatives thought hostile or at best indifferent to Jews. Israel became the flip side of the Holocaust; one coin would pair power with innocence in the years ahead.

Meeting Heschel and studying with Rubenstein in the early 1970s, I had little idea of what was coming. I thought I could carry the mandate for justice and the question of God together. I naively assumed that this combination could exist without much reflection. Though I knew I needed to reflect on each and constantly did so, it never occurred to me that these individual questions had to be dealt with as in fact two aspects of one question. Both Heschel and Rubenstein knew this.

Perhaps I understood at a deep level that taking either side of the coin would leave me unable to forge my own response in the post-Holocaust world. In retrospect, I think this was the trap into which my generation fell. Thus, we were unprepared, even for our failure to answer either question adequately. If the long sweep of Jewish history is any guide, our failure may have been inevitable.

Within a decade of Heschel's death, and with Rubenstein's most productive days behind him, the stakes of Jewish life escalated dramatically. It began with the aftermath of the great Israeli triumph in the 1967 Arab-Israeli war. The months before the war were filled with increasing tension. Israel struck decisively, achieving a lightning victory over the collective Arab countries in just six days. Jews, and much of the Western world, celebrated. Israel had struck a mighty blow for the defense of freedom and against the upstarts of the Third World. Israel was holding the fort for the retreating European empires and an America under siege in Vietnam. American Jews took this as a point of pride; the can-do spirit made us full Americans, but with a distinctive difference, our Jewishness. We celebrated this difference even as we became less and less different.

Almost all Jews were caught unaware in 1967, and to

this day many cannot understand where their own feelings lay. Still fewer can speak the terrible truth out loud. With what voice should we speak it? Who is there to listen and what will they hear? Herein lies the great and tragic Jewish conundrum.

Heschel had difficulty understanding such a moment in American history and the boost Israel's victory gave to American Jews. Though Heschel celebrated Israel's victory, he witnessed, and mourned, the loss of a Judaism that waned more and more after 1967 as the Holocaust and Israel became America's totemic Judaism. The God of history that had been psychologized and symbolized away left only a residue of action on behalf of justice in the wider world. The passing of the Jewish God had the immediate, but transient, effect of emphasizing the community's concentration on Jewish ethics. Perhaps social justice had been a substitute for God—the commitment of Jews in the 1950s and 1960s to the struggle for civil rights was palpable; but the later gains of Holocaust and Israel reined in this commitment. Intermittently, this Jewish residue of God could still embolden work for justice. When the immediate effect wore off, however, Jews were adrift. We remain so today.

Emphasizing Jewish suffering and power—as innocent and redemptive—made those who longed for a better world seem utopian. The only world we Jews could control was the extant world that was ours. Our efforts had to be concentrated within the Jewish community and a Jewish nation.

Just a little over a decade after the celebration of the 1967 victory, the Jewish community was rushing headlong

into a protracted siege. By the 1970s it was becoming clear
that the 1967 war had been a prelude to an expansionistic Israel that would displace Palestinians in Jerusalem and the
West Bank. Since the world was aware of Jewish suffering in
the Holocaust and residual anti-Semitism, it awaited word
from Jews themselves as to how to navigate these terrors. It
seemed almost impossible that a people who struggled and
suffered so much and who was grounded in a tradition that
resonated so profoundly with justice and compassion could
embark on and defend, almost without dissent, policies that
looked so much like the ones Jews had suffered from in the
past. The impossibility belied the reality.

True, criticism of Israel from non-Jews was increasing, a
sure danger for Jews and a country like Israel, which was dependent on outside support. More important, criticism from
within the Jewish community increased, first in small doses,
then exponentially. The Israeli invasion of Lebanon and subsequent bombing of Beirut in the 1980s served as a wake-up
call for Jews who were concerned about losing our ethical
compass. The crushing of the Palestinian uprising in the late
1980s and early 1990s had a similar impact. Israeli Jews,
aided and abetted by the American Jewish establishment,
mobilized to banish Jewish questioning to the margins of the
community. The force of this mobilization muzzled even the
more mainstream, moderate critics.

To the outside world, Israel's wars began looking more
and more like wars of choice. Once touted as an emergency
measure, the occupation of the West Bank and Gaza was now
decades old. Jerusalem, taken and forcibly united under Is-

raeli control in 1967, was being continually expanded so that it became part of a larger West Bank puzzle. Settlements planted within the occupied lands grew into fortified towns and cities.

When the Oslo Accords between Israel and the Palestinian Authority were signed in 1993, the facts on the ground were plain for anyone with focused eyes to see. Absent a forcible retreat to pre-1967 borders, Israel's occupation of Jerusalem and the West Bank was permanent.

The initial conquest of Palestine was expanding. The Israeli government had no intention of relinquishing part of its expanding state. Some of the land taken in 1967 and then in the October 1973 war was eventually handed back, Sinai and Gaza for example, but only in return for augmented territory and consolidation in Jerusalem and the West Bank.

Rubenstein judged Israel's behavior only on the basis of whether or not it enhanced Israel's security. The covenant with God had been broken in the Holocaust—where was God when we needed him most? Humanity had also broken its covenant with the Jewish people—where was humanity when Jews were being annihilated? So the only responsibility left for Jews was to protect and nourish ourselves.

Heschel, of course, had a different understanding and drew different conclusions. Though Jews faced difficult hurdles in history, the Holocaust being one, in the end, each of us was responsible to God. For Jews, ethical behavior was mandated toward both Jews and non-Jews alike.

The questions remained: Could Heschel's vision of Jewish life deal with this new historical phenomenon—Jews with a state of their own that had cleansed Palestinians from their homes and homeland? Could Heschel's vision deal with an Israel that kept expanding through wars and the oppression of another people in its struggle for freedom?

Rubenstein had a post-Holocaust sensibility that jettisoned a traditional ethical understanding in order for Jews to become and remain empowered. Heschel struggled to maintain a pre-Holocaust continuity with a Jewish understanding of justice in the post-Holocaust world. Heschel was disappointed by some of Israel's behavior. Could he understand and critique the basis of that behavior? Was Heschel's criticism of Israel symbolic, much like the symbolism used to define God, a view he so distrusted? Was Heschel's understanding of Israel a substitute for the real thing?

Heschel was controversial in his day, challenging the hypocrisy and lethargy of American Jews. He viewed the state of Israel through the lenses of his Eastern European Judaism, the beauty of the Sabbath, and the Jewish longing for a renewed presence in the Holy Land. With that background, it is doubtful that Heschel could have risen to the occasion when the stakes became higher, with Jews dealing out suffering rather than absorbing it. Could Heschel have found the courage to criticize Israel and its increasing militancy? Heschel died before the Lebanon war and Israel's brutal repression of the Palestinian uprisings in the last decades of the twentieth century. Heschel was also spared experiencing and commenting on the permanent occupation, settlements, and control of the West Bank. But Heschel had experienced the formation of Israel and the expulsion of the Palestinians. On this, the creation of Israel, he said little.[3]

If Heschel had lived and spoken out, there is little question that his stature in the Jewish community would have fallen precipitately. The symbolic power of the Holocaust and Israel would have been too much to counter, even for so great a thinker and leader. If he had spoken out he would have been exiled from the mainstream of the Jewish community and joined the ranks of other Jews similarly treated. Would that have moved his Diaspora experience, so haunted by the Holocaust, into exile? Driven from Europe, would he have also been driven from America?

In the 1980s I began to realize that neither Heschel's understanding nor Rubenstein's was enough to address the crisis Jews had entered. If it was true that contemporary Jewish identity came *after* the Holocaust, it was also true that Jewish identity came *after* Israel and *after* Israel's innocence with regard to the Palestinian people.

Heschel's God demanded justice: could that justice be applied to us? Rubenstein's God was power: could we pursue that God and still call ourselves Jews?

A GODLESS JUDAISM?

As I entered public life in the 1980s I reached a crossroads quite similar to that of other Jews. By now the Holocaust was firmly fixed in our minds and hearts. What had begun as an internal Jewish issue was now important in the wider public arena. The conduit for the public airing of the Holocaust was Rubenstein at first, with articles about his views appearing in the *New York Times* and in a *Playboy* interview. By the 1980s, however, Rubenstein's influence was fading.

Rubenstein's place was taken by a new Holocaust star, Elie Wiesel, whose autobiographical *Night*, published in English in the 1960s, detailed his experiences in Auschwitz. Wiesel's book justifiably took the country by storm, but his elevation startled the Jewish establishment. For reasons of self-preservation, it had stonewalled discussion of the Holocaust in the 1950s and early 1960s. Quite correctly, the establishment feared that if Holocaust consciousness became dominant, a new Jewish establishment would rise in its place.[4]

Wiesel's meteoric ascent startled everyone, himself included. He had barely survived in Auschwitz as he watched his mother and sister disappear in the gas chambers and his father die before his eyes. His fame could hardly be explained in any rational way. Wiesel's rise coincided with the building of the Holocaust Memorial Museum in Washington, D.C. The idea for the museum began in the 1970s and culminated with its opening in 1993. Wiesel was the first chair of the council that oversaw the building of the museum, appropriately so, since the museum was largely created through the influence of his writing in the Jewish and Christian communities in the United States.

The idea of the Holocaust as a formative event quickly permeated the Jewish community. By the mid-1980s the Holocaust had become Americanized; it was a lesson to all humanity about the historic suffering of Jews and the beacon of light that America was in a world filled with darkness. It elevated figures within the Jewish world beyond their analytical and emotional capacities. Soon Wiesel was called upon to comment on political and intellectual events around the world, even before he was awarded the Nobel Peace Prize in 1986. As a Nobel laureate, Wiesel was asked to comment on an array of world issues. But the range of his knowledge was narrow, and his thinking was not systematic. Often, Wiesel seemed confused and unable to speak directly to the issues at hand.

A subtext of the Holocaust museum is Israel. Israel's survival and flourishing are a sign of the light surviving the darkness, implying that as Israel goes, so goes humanity. With America at Israel's side, the future appears bright indeed. Like Israel, America also represents the golden age of a resurgent world Jewry. Thus, the location of the Holocaust museum on the Mall in Washington, D.C., symbolizes this new age.

Because of the increasing power of the Holocaust idea and of the American Jewish community, the fact that this was the only historical experience represented on the Mall that was not, historically at least, American caused little if any comment. Paradoxically, overcoming this event of mass death on European soil represented the triumph of American Jews and by extension of Israel. The Holocaust museum celebrates Israel as part of the American experience, too.

When Wiesel was relatively unknown, he and Heschel were friends; they often spent the Sabbath walking and talking on New York's Upper West Side. They shared memories of Eastern Europe and the Holocaust, could speak to each other in Yiddish, and were similarly displaced in America. Their views on the Holocaust and God were not the same, however, and after Heschel died and Wiesel ascended in the Jewish and American imagination, Wiesel's views diverged from Heschel's.

A comparison between the two helps us grasp the evolving understanding of Jews in America. Heschel played down the significance of the Holocaust in relation to Judaism and God. Despite the agony involved for Heschel and his family, Heschel did not see the Holocaust as causing a fundamental break within the Jewish framework of belief and life. For Heschel, halacha, Jewish law, remained in place, as did divine sovereignty. While Hasidic life permeated Heschel's worldview, he spoke in a modern and American idiom. His nostalgia for the Jewish past was balanced by the sense that Eastern Europe was lost. The bridge between the two worlds was a living Judaism that emphasized God and the prophetic. Israel, the state, was involved in Heschel's equation but only as a reality dependent on the foundations of God and justice that Heschel felt defined Jewish life. Heschel was a Diaspora Jew, and for him, the state of Israel could be in exile too, if God was absent and Judaism was trivialized.

Heschel wrote little about the practical realities of Israel. Wiesel also writes little about Israel, though he often speaks in Israel's defense. However, Wiesel's comments, mostly without direct reference to actual events taking place there, are of a different nature than Heschel's. God has little if any place in Wiesel's lexicon concerning Israel, pro or con. For Wiesel, Israel is the new absolute, untouchable by others and by Jews themselves. Virtually no critique is permitted, save the speech of Israelis within certain boundaries.

This silence on Israel comports with Wiesel's sense that after Auschwitz, there can be little if any direct speech about God. Therefore speech about God, too, is limited. The internal prophetic critique of Jewish power, latent in Heschel, is absent from Wiesel.

This lack of critique holds for another Holocaust theologian, Orthodox rabbi Irving Greenberg, who also believes that God was absent in Auschwitz. Because of God's absence, what Jews need now is power. For Greenberg, Jewish power is mandated in light of the Holocaust but endangered by the prophetic. Jews are experts in exercising the prophetic and have done so ably and appropriately when Jews have been without power. With Jews having power the prophetic becomes dangerous, especially as it relates to Israel's existence. No nation can withstand the prophetic if its critique is rigorously applied. In this sense, Israel, the state, is like any other state. Does that mean that Jews are like other peoples?[5]

Wiesel's popularity lies in his answer to Greenberg's question. From the 1970s on Wiesel has mediated the sensibility that Jews are different and that Israel, the state, unlike other nations, is innocent. The reason that Israel is innocent is because Jews have suffered, especially during the Holocaust, so that Jews are, ipso facto, very nearly incapable of causing suffering. The particularity of Jews comes from the original covenant, which includes God, the Land, and the prophetic.

Since neither God nor the prophetic can be vouched for or voiced after the Holocaust, the Land is the repository of what remains of the Promise given ancient Israel. The Promise was tainted by the Holocaust; Israel, the state, is the place where what is left of the Promise remains. America is the protector of the Promise. Therefore America and American Jews are innocent as well.

Wiesel's narrative of Jewish history is part biblical, part European, part Hasidic, and part American. In all parts of this narrative, the prophetic is diminished in lieu of Jewish suffering and the dream of survival and peace. Unlike Heschel and, in another way, Rubenstein, Wiesel narrates a story of suffering and redemption unmediated by politics or ideology. Jewhatred and Jew-love are the two engines of history. Holocaust is the nadir of that history, Israel its possible redemption.

The role of God in Wiesel is much closer to Rubenstein than to Heschel. Though Wiesel has a severe and unrelenting argument with Rubenstein over tone and the banishment of the covenant, their views regarding God's absence are similar. What Wiesel and Rubenstein argue about to the end is the future of the Jewish people. Unlike Wiesel, Rubenstein sees little future for Judaism and the Jewish people. Without God and the covenant, why continue? Here Heschel and Rubenstein are much closer at least in foundational outlook about the need for God. They simply see the continuing reality of God quite differently.

To live through the development of Holocaust theology was to live through a shift in Jewish consciousness. Being at this intersection also meant seeing aspects of this consciousness within myself. Being at the intersection was also to be rent asunder. I could no longer accept part of what was known and accepted as Jewish. For some thinkers, if Jews did not accept this new post-Holocaust definition of Jewishness, we ceased to be Jewish.

Illustrative of this dilemma was a new sense of power. Coming of age in the 1960s and early 1970s, I did not know a Jew with a low self-image of him- or herself. Nor did I know a Jew who didn't enjoy being Jewish or assert that Jewishness when appropriate. Every Jew I knew was aware of anti-Semitism. No Jew I knew thought anti-Semitism defined our world or limited our opportunities in life.

Paradoxically, in this brave new world, where Jewish self-assertion was translated into the need to have and protect power, a new Jewish emphasis on anti-Semitism arose. The anti-Semitism I had known as a child, mostly through distant stories or personal slights, was transformed. It became an essential aspect of Holocaust thought that emphasized the state of Israel as central to Jewish existence. Holocaust consciousness saw anti-Semitism shifting from the European form of denying rights to Jewish citizens within national boundaries to the denial of Jewish particularity and its empowerment in the state of Israel. By the 1980s, with dissent toward Israel accelerating in the international community and among Jews, opposition to Israeli policies vis-à-vis the Palestinians became the focal point of what was alternately termed the "real" or "new" anti-Semitism. Whatever individuals thought of Jews, the new anti-Semitism was defined as the denial of the right of Israel to exist as Jewish state.[6]

Critiques of Zionism—the assertion of Jewish destiny in Israel—and any form of organized political or religious solidarity with Palestinians asserting a right to their own state were also defined as anti-Semitic. In this redefinition, bodies as diverse as the United Nations and the World Council of Churches were defined as anti-Semitic. Included also were movements in the Third World that saw Israel as part and parcel of Western colonialism in world history.

Members of the Jewish establishment had little patience with these criticisms from a varied and struggling world. Any group or movement that identified Israel with the politics of injustice or colonialism was branded with a Holocaustian view as anti-Semitic. Rather than being considered a principled opposition that could be listened to, aspects of which could be affirmed or denied, even nuanced ethical criticisms were often simply rejected outright. The criticisms came to symbolize—with dire consequences—the plight of Jews both without and with power: The world hunts Jews when we are without power and when we have power. If Jews aren't vigilant, these anti-Semitic forces will subsume us in the fires of another Holocaust. Holocaust consciousness became oriented toward the future rather than the past, and the stakes increased, as did the warnings.

Jewish memory is profoundly attuned to formative events in history. The Holocaust was activated to remember for the future. The warning of Holocaust memory could work two ways: as a warning against atrocity and mass death happening again to Jews and indeed to any people; or, and primarily, as a warning to Jews that mass death was around the corner for Jews and hence logically for Israel. Though Holocaust consciousness initially contained both warnings, over time, the latter became emphasized to the exclusion of the first. Jews were on the firing line; Israel was the trip wire.

Jewish empowerment in America and Israel introduced a new level of anxiety among Jews. With no power to lose, we needed power. As we gained power, we feared losing it. Both our previous lack of power and our newly achieved power were analyzed within the broad sweep of Jewish history. The politics of power was subsumed in the dramatic story of an ancient suffering people that had emerged on the world stage with a state of its own. Since Jewish power was not analyzed as being achieved through a political process, Jews found it difficult to understand the politics in and around the state when exercised by power brokers with different histories and interests.

When Jews see themselves as cosmic actors on a universal stage, those who critique aspects of Jewish power find themselves in the Jewish existential drama. Therefore, Palestinians are no longer people with a political existence, but players in the drama of Jewish destiny. Jews have rarely affirmed their grievances as political in nature. In few places in Jewish post-Holocaust literature do we find a reckoning with Palestinians as a collective and political entity. As individuals, Palestinians may be in difficult straits; Jews might empathize with a displaced Palestinian, but the collective aspirations of

the Palestinian people, as a people or national entity, politi-
cize their circumstances. If indeed Palestinians have political
rights, if the individual plight of the Palestinians can be addressed only within a political framework, then Jewish empowerment is also political, to be supported or opposed on
purely political grounds.

Politicizing the Israeli-Palestinian conflict levels the
playing field and introduces new variables. Jewish empowerment might be absolutely necessary considering the prior
conditions of the Jews of Europe. The question remains
whether the only way of ensuring this empowerment is
through a Jewish state in the Middle East. If because of Jewish history and the recent and historical experience of mis-
treatment of Jews as a minority community within Europe, a
Jewish state is deemed necessary, can that be justified if another people must lose their own homeland? Since Israel
came into being through the displacement of hundreds of
thousands of Palestinians, what responsibility do Jews have
to them as we seek to secure our own future? If only the political is emphasized, can Jews justify gaining security at the
expense of another people?

If the emergency situation after the Holocaust meant el-
evating Jews above others to achieve what the Jewish community needed, is there not a concomitant responsibility
when the emergency is over to redress the grievances of
those displaced? Political and religious communities hardly
ever agree on aspirations and needs, but without having to
agree with every criticism of Israel or any other political entity, it would seem incumbent on those with power to address

the needs of those on the other side of their unjust uses of power.

Heschel's warning against a Godless Jewishness was prescient. By distancing ourselves from the foundations of what it means to be a Jew, we are left with self-assertion without a radical critique of our own actions. Power for power's sake—Rubenstein's formula and in his mind the absent politics we needed in the Holocaust—was achieved in the decades after the Holocaust. Such consolidated Jewish power lacks a reference point within and outside itself to make judgments about its path and scope. Any attempt to discuss that power outside its dimensions, as defined by Jews, is deemed outside Jewish discourse and against Jews as a collective.

Raising the specter of a "new" anti-Semitism limits the world's ability to speak truth to Jewish power. It also warns Jews against the prophetic as a form of self-hate, the other side of the new anti-Semitism. In sum, the prophetic critique of Jewish power is defined as in league with the organized and unorganized anti-Semites of the world. Treason against Jews—the very prospect of another Holocaust—is deemed to come from outside and also from within.

The evolution of this understanding occurred well before September 11 and the flood of new invectives on the subject of the "new" anti-Semitism that followed. The 1990s saw the Jewish community in a holding pattern. Nothing new had come from the commentators on the Holocaust for some years. This was quite understandable, because this path of analysis had become exhausted.

The 1993 Oslo process failed; by 2000 a new Palestinian

uprising was in full swing, with the forces used against it magnified from the first uprising. During the first uprising, Israel's army used the policy of breaking bones and mass incarceration of protestors. By the turn of the millennium, Israel's military was using helicopter gunships and political assassinations as its weapons of choice. Israel was also using collective punishment—closing towns and cities and building the Separation Wall within Palestinian territory—as a strategy of choice.

Other differences fed a further downward spiral in the standoff between Israel and the Palestinians. During the first uprising there was an amazing amount of cross-border exchange, with many Israelis and Palestinians joining together to aid the injured and to work together for a two-state solution. Although there was plenty of violence, with many permanently injured and scores dead—the overwhelming majority of these Palestinians—there was a muted hope that through this struggle a new path could be born. By the time of the second uprising, even this hope was banished. The promise of Oslo faded; the ever-expanding Jewish settlements in the West Bank had become large towns and small cities. The Separation Wall in Jerusalem and the West Bank was under construction. This shifted the argument about Israel's designs and Palestinian possibility from the hope for a two-state solution to whether or not Israeli policy was legitimate to prevent suicide bombers from reaching inside Israel. For many Palestinians—and some Jews as well—the building of the wall sealed the Palestinian population into enclaves. Some called them Bantustans. Others dared to say "ghettos."

An apartheid system was evolving or being consolidated, depending on one's perspective; the moral arguments of Holocaust theology and Jewish dissent had quieted. After these many years, what could dissenters say that hadn't been said before and failed? The Jewish establishment found it too difficult to make the Holocaust argument any longer. What was left was the anti-Semitism of the "Arabs." After September 11, Israel and the American Jewish establishment became intertwined with the United States–declared "war on terror."

The Palestinians were seen as part and parcel of that terror, making Israel, once again, as it had been in 1967, a Western bulwark. This time, a militant Islam was in the forefront of America's concerns, and the Jewish community took up this clarion call with alacrity. With the United States reeling from terrorist attacks on its own soil, many in the American Jewish establishment felt that now ordinary Americans would "understand" at a deeper level what Israel had been "dealing with" for years.

The second Palestinian uprising, like the first, was also destroyed. But this time there was little hope left at the end of the struggle. Instead, there was an ever-growing sense of pessimism. The expansion of Israel was ongoing. Was it permanent? The Palestinians had suffered such losses of life and land over the previous decades that their national movement was in tatters. There seemed little hope of its resurrection.

Jewish dissent diminished. Since Israelis died in greater number during the second uprising (though Palestinian casualties still far outnumbered those of Israelis), progressive Jewish movements such as the Israeli Peace Now were virtually silent. Jewish voices for peace were caught short when Palestinians took their own struggle into Israel. Palestinians dared to say a huge *no* to Israel and began to say, loudly and clearly, that even progressive Jews were part of their problem. This surprised progressive Jews. Citing again and again the power of the Jewish ethical tradition to hold Jewish power accountable, but retaining elements of a patronizing and limited view of what indeed could change the situation, progressive Jews were stymied. The ground of discussion and action had shifted.

After September 11, much of the Jewish Left abandoned the Left. The question that remained was whether the Jewish Left had ever truly been Left. Was the mainstream of Jewish dissent a barely disguised pseudoalternative to the Jewish establishment? In fact their arguments, seemingly so disparate, essentially repeated each other; they were expressions of Jewish ascendancy in America and Israel, though couched in different terms. It was at this time that I began to wonder whether the problem was contemporary Jewishness itself, or the argument from Jewishness, however articulated.

In retrospect, the trajectory can be clearly seen: the formation of a Constantinian Judaism, progressive Jews becoming, intentionally or not, its left wing. This meant that opposition to the establishment was merely rhetorical. The hypocrisy of it all was unnerving. Jews and Judaism seemed parked in a dark alley. The way to move forward, if there was one, was obscured.

After September 11 and the crushing of the second uprising, I knew that the only way forward for Palestinians would be with their abject surrender. That seemed to be the reason for the electoral victory of Hamas in the Palestinian elections of 2006 after the death of Yasir Arafat in 2004. This was before the second Lebanon war, which occurred in the summer of 2006, another war of attrition calculated to reverse Lebanon's development for another decade or two. To survive in its present configuration, Israel needed the Arab world around it, including the Palestinian territories, to be constantly de-developed. Economic, social, and political advancement threatened Israeli superiority in the region; its survival was calculated on the underdevelopment of its Middle Eastern neighbors.

The backwardness and corruption of the Arab societies and governments had been touted for decades, a not so subtle subtheme of Holocaust theology. It was a backwardness that was endemic and of long standing. Could it also be, as the subtext inferred, inherent?

Jews historically bore ignominy through the racialized bigotry at play in what was deliberately referred to as the "Jewish Question." That bigotry had now morphed into the "Arab Question," a formulation long embedded in Western consciousness and linked historically to Islam. Now its transmogrification was lodged in Jewish consciousness as well as in Jewish arguments. September 11 exacerbated the vehemence of these racial understandings.

It amazed me how Jews of high intellectual caliber internalized this racism. In many ways it pervaded progressive Jewish thinking as much as it did that of the Constantinian Jewish establishment. In progressive Jewish life most of these racist understandings were mouthed in paternalistic slogans that made Israel's security paramount. Palestinians and Arabs needed to guarantee that security, first by accepting Israel's right to exist as a Jewish state, and second by agreeing that an emerging Palestinian state would not develop or maintain any armed forces. To add insult to injury, the Palestinians' obvious need for protection would be answered by Israel's army. The Israel Defense Forces would patrol the borders of Palestine.

This, then, was the progressive understanding of the solution to the Israeli-Palestinian conflict: Israel would keep its conquered lands, including Jerusalem and most of the settlements in the West Bank. Palestine would accept its conquered status, reducing its land claim to roughly 22 percent of historic Palestine—minus East Jerusalem and the land now occupied by the Jewish settlements around Jerusalem—while pledging to exist within borders controlled by Israel. Palestine would exist side by side with an Israel that was economically, politically, and militarily superior. Good behavior might be rewarded in the future, though the rewards had inherent limitations in Palestine's neighbors. I couldn't help but think that this system was a recipe for a Palestine continually dependent on Israel and thus for Palestine's continued de-development.

The argument from progressive Jews, and sometimes

from the Constantinian establishment as well, was that this no-win system was likely the best deal the Palestinians would receive. Jews of all stripes were amazed that Palestinians continually rejected these "generous" offers. This rejection confirmed for many Jews that something was inherently amiss in the Palestinian and Arab psyche. These people were unable to recognize a logical, reasonable, and "fair" offer.

The 2006 Lebanon war clearly reintroduced the dilemma Jews faced. Israel's bombardment of Lebanon was relentless, even as internal Israeli dissent over the handling of the war mounted. At the same time, Hezbollah rockets consistently hit Israel. Lebanon was burning; so was Israel. Watching the war from afar, I could imagine Israel being one rocket away from destruction. An atomic payload delivered into Tel Aviv, or a number of rockets with less payload, could spell the end of Israel and its population. The distances in the Middle East are small. Modern technology erases boundaries. Jewish authorities were correct in saying that one lapse in defense could mean the demise of millions of Jews.

Herein lies the deepest quandary of Jewish thought. Whatever one thinks of the policies of the state of Israel, millions of Jews live within its borders. The danger to Jews is there, ethical and physical. Like other states, Israel often violates the ethics of justice; such violations are detrimental to the future of the Jewish people. The state also embodies the physical danger inherent in a small expansionist state. Ethically, culturally, and theologically, Jews are left with a state that few of its own Jewish citizens, let alone millions of Jews outside the state, control.

Ironically, the Jewish people who gave birth to Israel now take a backseat to its power. Jews are left to argue and sometimes to die for state policies that are decided, as in most states, by a few politicians in league with a small and powerful elite. Judaism and Jewish life are, thus, hostage to the state of Israel and its politicians.

I remember well Rubenstein's insistence on the flawed nature of Jewish leadership from Roman times to the Holocaust. Judaism, in its rabbinic formulation, began with the defeat of the Jews in Jerusalem at the hands of the Romans in 70 and 124 C.E. Jewish leadership struck a deal with the Romans to let a Jewish remnant survive and flourish if Jews would accept a minority, demilitarized presence within larger, dominant host communities. This deal determined Jewish destiny for almost two thousand years. By accepting this minority status, Jews developed leadership patterns that emphasized compromise, bribery, and, when safety was most threatened, flight, since Jews had no military means to defend ourselves.[7]

This deal allowed Judaism and separate Jewish communities to survive, prompting Rubenstein to analyze rather than blame Jewish leadership. However, it also meant that Jewish leaders failed to perceive the shifting power and objectives that the Nazis represented. Jewish leaders thought that the old tried and true tactics of Jewish survival during difficult times would suffice to placate the Nazis. Rubenstein believed Jewish leaders woke up to the Nazi challenge far too late because the patterns of Jewish life made it impossible for them to comprehend the threat of total annihilation. Hence,

Rubenstein regards as understandable the lesson of the Holocaust: Jews must use power to defend Jewish life at any cost. If Jews do go down again, at least this time they will take their enemies down with them.

To prevent mass death in the Middle East, Jewish and non-Jewish, we are faced with the question of where Jewish power is leading us. Could Jewish leaders, heeding the lessons of the Holocaust, be leading us to the brink of another, perhaps prouder, destruction? Schooled in the lessons of the Holocaust and the clear failures of the rabbinic sensibility, are they leading us, this time with power, to another Holocaust?

SEARCHING FOR MY *OTHER* VOICE

Jews were historically schooled in the abuse of state power against us. Despite this schooling, when it came to us, we felt there would be a difference. The Jewish tradition of ethical concern would be strong enough to discipline Jewish power. Like most Jews, I felt the strength of my tradition. As it turns out, Jews were wrong. So was I. The conundrum for Jews who support a state that is outside of our control may be common to all peoples and traditions. All states may be outside of the people's control. Still, all power needs an ethical accounting. Is there something about the Jewish tradition that is lacking, or does the Jewish tradition stand in relation to power as any religious and or cultural tradition does—as the weakest part of the ethic-versus-power equation?

I first traveled to Israel in response to a Hebrew-school teacher's admonition. After the 1967 war, I read about a new

Palestinian refugee crisis the war had precipitated. Since it was in a national newsweekly, I thought he would know about it. He was so angry at my question that he started yelling at me. Right then and there I decided that if I ever had a chance to see the situation for myself I would.

I went to Israel in 1973. Touring it, I immediately noticed a disparity between Jews—mostly of European background—and Arabs, as Palestinians were primarily known at the time. For the most part, I noticed a difference of color, a difference Jews of my generation were quite attuned to because of the civil rights movement. I also noticed distinctive cultural differences between the European sensibility of Israeli Jews and the Middle Eastern sensibility of the Arabs. Because I had experienced the first, the second sensibility felt like otherness to me. I remember the Old City of Jerusalem as distinctly Arab and different. Even though Israel conquered East Jerusalem in 1967 and annexed it immediately afterward, the city had yet to experience the shift to its contemporary character. Today the Old City is primarily Jewish.

Carrying Heschel and Rubenstein within me as I traversed Israel for a month, I carried my American sensitivities as well. Like most Jews of that time, I knew little of the history of the emergence of the state of Israel and the displacement of the Palestinians. What I carried was a romanticized sense of Israel's return to the Land and its lightning victory in the 1967 war.

Like most American Jews, I had celebrated Israel's victory as if I were on the battlefield with the Israeli soldiers.

Likewise, I had enjoyed the jokes circulating at the time about the poorly trained and cowardly Arab soldiers. In these jokes there was a racial and cultural component that makes me queasy today. But then, I did not notice the implication of such jokes—even though just decades earlier, similar stereotypes of Jews had provided a basis for the psychological distancing that the Nazis needed to carry out their persecution. My encounter with Israel and the Palestinians in 1973 was earthshaking in the long run. At that point, however, I had no idea of what to do with this experience. Clearly "white" Jews were on top in Israel, "colored" Palestinians on the bottom.

Later, the great Palestinian scholar Edward Said identified this sense of the "otherness" of the Arab Palestinians as "Orientalism." In the 1990s, I came to know Said, and through our meetings, I began to look back on my early encounters with Palestinians with reference to my European and American background. Yet there was also another, latent dimension in my meeting with the Palestinian other. Was this Palestinian other also an avenue to discover the Jewish other to my Jewishness? This second part of the other, my own, would take years for me to understand and more time to articulate.[8]

Since our Hebrew-school education had given Jews in 1973 little if any historical background on Israel or the Palestinians, what I viewed in person was like a piece of art in a museum without the details of the artist or the conceptual understanding of the art. There was injustice, but who created it? I saw and felt that injustice. The difference was that Jews created this situation. How did this come to pass and what could be done about it? My questions were compounded by the fact that during the month I toured Israel—October—another war began. On Yom Kippur, the Jewish Day of Atonement, I was touring the old city of Acre on the Mediterranean Sea. I walked by the synagogues and saw Jews outside draped with talliths listening to transistor radios. The war had begun earlier in the day. The Yom Kippur worshippers were listening for general news about the war as well as specific instructions for their unit call-ups.

The streets of Acre were remarkably quiet. Once the troops were mobilized and the military equipment was moved to the various fronts, I had an overwhelming sense that a people's destiny hung in the balance. Israelis I met exuded confidence; they also admitted that a defeat would be the end of everything, including their lives. It was like an out-of-body experience. I was in their war zone too, but I felt like an observer. I wondered if this would be like the 1967 war, with a quick and decisive victory, or if this would be a different kind of war, one that dragged on for weeks, perhaps months, with the outcome hanging long in the balance.

What was an American Jew to take away from this war? Israel's victory in the 1973 war did not repeat its 1967 victory. Egypt's surprise attack was successful, and the larger threat was beaten back only after many Israeli casualties and the loss of territory. The United States shipped arms to Israel to keep Israel from using tactical nuclear weapons. In 1973, Israel was on the brink of survival. That reality made it more difficult for me to search out the complexities of the political and religious issues involved, both as a human being and as a Jew.

Regardless of who was right or wrong, I asked whether an American Jew could afford to analyze critically Israel's founding and existence. American social justice in the civil rights movement might serve as a model for Israel and the Palestinians during peacetime. I wasn't sure it could apply when war threatened the very existence of Jews living within a Jewish state.

What was my responsibility toward these Jews? Though nothing in the Jewish world that I knew suggested it, I also wondered if I had a responsibility toward Israel's other, the Palestinians. My mind was torn. My kinship with Jews was obviously foremost; to see the injustices against Palestinians might require me to abandon that kinship in favor of a more disinterested judgment. With my own people on the line, transcending background and loyalties could be seen as treasonous. To be responsible for both, I needed a framework to work this out in my mind and on the ground. To say that this framework was distant is an understatement. As far as I knew, it didn't exist. My experience had little reference point or detail, since I had neither read anything nor met anyone with a dissenting view on Israel. My time in Israel aroused complex feelings with no resolution.

I spent the next decade finishing my studies and living and working among the poor in New York, Atlanta, and New Orleans. These experiences expanded but also further complicated my relation to Judaism and the Jewish community. My time spent with the poor in the United States and abroad, as well as my experience of the spirituality of Christian movements among the poor, provided experiences that both confirmed and contradicted my understanding of the Holocaust and what I had learned in Israel. In relation to the affluence of most American Jews, the lives of the poor seemed a world apart and different from Jewish life. Where would these experiences take me as a person and a Jew? I hoped that someday these experiences would help me sort out my own Jewishness. How this would work and where I would land, I was unsure.

It isn't unusual to have to leave one's own world in order to see life from another perspective. While I worked with the poor without giving it much thought, I had an intuitive sense that the only way I could be faithful as a Jew would be by leaving the community for a time. Something was happening within Jewish life that made it difficult, if not impossible, to see clearly where Jews as a community were heading. The difficulty was how to articulate the problems with what was happening and change direction.

Those Jewish leaders who sought a new affiliation in the United States with the powerful outside Judaism were increasingly defining Jewish identity. These leaders saw their communal responsibility as positioning our community with the powerful. Jews needed and deserved our own place in the fabric of society and the world, like other communities. Still, Jewish history told us that there was more to life than power. While assuring our flourishing, aligning with the elite often consigned others to the margins. I had seen this in Israel, manifest in a set of policies that privileged Jews over others. The Jewish community in America was heading in that direction as well. What sensibilities and proposals could help us change course was unclear.

I found guidance from Professor William Miller, a historian of the South and a southerner, but a sense of clarity about that change would take many years to form. Miller influenced me in my university days as profoundly as Rubenstein. Miller became involved with the Catholic Worker movement and subsequently wrote the first history of the movement and the first biography of its founder, Dorothy Day.[9]

Miller, like Rubenstein, was somewhat eclectic and eccentric; two more different personalities would be hard to find. Rubenstein defined his boundaries in an assertive and sometimes belligerent way, but he always invited and respected opinions different from his own. Miller was quiet and rarely announced his point of view. He refused to respond to questions asked of him if they related to the formation of another person's conscience.

A year after I visited Israel, I graduated from college, then flew to New York City, where I lived at the Catholic Worker house for a year. True to the movement's principles, "volunteers," as we were called, lived and worked among the poor in houses of hospitality. Here the poor were fed and housed. Though Catholic in its inspiration, the Catholic Worker was quite different from some Christian charitable organizations like the Salvation Army. No religious obligations were forced on those who came for help. Nor were there programs to help them to reintegrate into society.

The Catholic Worker was shaped by and in turn lived out

a radical Catholic message, which included a critique of modern industrial capitalist society. Catholics, such as Jacques Maritain, and non-Catholics, such as Mohandas Gandhi and Martin Buber, had issued such critiques. Led by the charismatic Dorothy Day, the Catholic Worker lived out these critiques through a communal life whose foundation was spiritual. In so doing, the Worker practiced a criticism of American society, where the "haves" ruled the "have-nots" and poverty was inflicted on many while the few enjoyed the spoils of an unjust division of resources.

The Catholic Worker drew upon diverse religious and intellectual traditions. Though ecumenical and interfaith in aspects of its thought and outreach, the Worker's foundational driving force was a radical interpretation of Catholicism. A controversial example was Dorothy Day's pacifist stand during World War II. At first glance her pacifism was at odds with the just-war tradition of the Roman Catholic Church. Respectful of that tradition, Day critically evaluated whether modern warfare allowed for the distinctions that the just-war tradition mandated. She and the Worker movement found that modern warfare, with its indiscriminate violence, did not meet the test.

At the same time that the Catholic Worker applied just-war ideas in an unusual way, it also counseled the immediate and unconditional acceptance of Jewish refugees from Nazi Europe into America. Thus, while opposed to World War II, the Worker modified traditional Catholic sensibilities toward Jews. Emblazoned on the front page of its newspaper were illustrations with expressive captions, noting the Jewishness of Jesus and asserting that harm done to Jews was an injury to Jesus.

At the Worker, I lived among the poor and saw their faces as they lined up outside the doors each morning for soup and bread. It was a life-changing experience. Suffering in present-day America burrowed deep inside of me. The images remain vivid to me today. Homeless men and women, some driven to the streets because of financial difficulties and others beset by deep-seated psychological problems, seemed helpless and driven to a despair I found almost impossible to imagine.

Few, if any, of the folks on that soup line were Jewish. The Jewish America I grew up in was quite different from the America I witnessed in my time in New York City. Some years earlier Michael Harrington, a democratic socialist and a former volunteer at the Catholic Worker, saw this soup line as part of the "Other America." As a Jew, I experienced this Other America, and I felt responsible for the lives I saw. I understood that I was living within a system that created tremendous wealth for the few, among whom were many Jews, and dislocation and despair for too many. Was this in any way like the Palestinian otherness I had just experienced?

There were still other Americas. These I witnessed in Atlanta the following summer and in New Orleans the year after I did further study. In both cities I worked with poor Blacks in their history of suffering and struggle for civil rights and equal opportunities. In Atlanta I visited massive public housing projects on the outskirts of the city. Nearly self-contained entities, they had their own schools and public services within walking distance of the projects. I could see that the aim was to keep this poor population away from the more affluent sectors of Atlanta. The projects appeared to me as ghettos like the segregated precincts in which European Jews had been forced to live. These projects were an updated and Americanized strategy for dealing with a subjugated and superfluous population.

Rubenstein had warned that the European Jewish experience was a paradigm for the twentieth century. Hence, the Holocaust was paradigmatic for other peoples in the twentieth century and beyond. Segregation was the first step in a process that separated and ultimately denied Jews their legal and political rights. This process stripped Jews of the protection of the state and left Jews vulnerable to the forces that sought their destruction. I felt I was witnessing a similar process, however modified, of segregation and denial. As a post-Holocaust Jew, I asked what my responsibilities were.

New Orleans was more of the same, though with a distinctive New Orleans accent. I worked in the St. Thomas Projects adjacent to the upscale Garden District. Unlike the Atlanta projects, here poverty and wealth existed side by side. Perhaps because of this proximity, the contrast revealing injustice was even greater. I worked to provide public platforms for poor Black women to tell their stories about issues that mattered most to them. I had taught them a little Black history. It was a rudimentary introduction, to be sure, but since these women had never studied their own history, a basic history allowed them to fit their own personal and family experience into a broader narrative. They spoke of their views on welfare, the police, health care, and the public schools, as well as their sense of Black history, where they had come from, where they were going.

To make sense of the broader arc of their history, I presented Black history within the schema of formative events, events that helped to shape the orientation, disorientation, and reorientation of a people's journey through time. It was, perhaps, a too obvious pattern: Africa as their origin, slavery as their crucible, and the civil rights movement as their possibility. Hearing their own story rehearsed within a larger context gave these women hope that their life struggles had a meaning beyond difficulty and failure. Their notion of personal failure underwent a conscious reversal. The long march to freedom was long indeed. They were a link in a chain that would grow stronger with time. The Promised Land that Martin Luther King Jr. spoke about so eloquently became part of their mission. If they didn't reach that land, as King didn't, perhaps their children would. Women who had just emerged from the sharecropping system embraced this history and this hope; their history was exciting and meaningful to them. It was also important to me.

The women who brought me to New Orleans were Catholic sisters. The sisters lived out of a Vatican II sensibility, which said the Church had to come closer to the people in service, for the Church *was* the people. Involvement in the world was a charism that faithful Christians were enjoined to live fully. As part of an evolving Vatican II spirituality, living with the poor was a privilege and an obligation, a work of mercy. As Jesus did in his ministry, Catholics were called upon to do the same. Though without the rigorous political understanding that the Catholic Worker possessed, this small group of Catholic sisters lived in the projects as a testimony to their faith lived out in the world.

The Christian spiritualities of the Catholic women and of the Black churches were quite different. The Christianity I found in the Black churches was so distinct that it suggested another faith altogether. Though the texts used came from the same canonical books and the claims of Jesus's divinity were invoked on all sides, I sensed a division between the white and Black churches that was deeper than worship and preaching style. I asked myself whether I was experiencing the same Christian faith celebrated in different idioms, or witnessing, as an outsider Jew, two different faiths, one further away and the other closer to my own faith as a Jew. This helped prepare me for understanding that division among Jews might be more than a surface division.

It might seem strange that the juxtaposition of the two Christian faith communities raised questions about my own Jewish faith. Like most of my generation, I didn't consider my own Jewishness a faith at all. Instead I saw it as an inherited and ingrained identity, to be practiced rather than believed. Still, I began to think of Christian differences in relation to my own Jewish difference. The Vatican II spirituality I experienced in New York and New Orleans was complemented by parts of the Black church spirituality I experienced in New Orleans. Though I admired the spirituality of the Vatican II Catholics, I felt more at home in a Black church.

I noticed immediately that the Exodus was spur to the Black struggle today and that slavery, seen as a countertestimony to the promised liberation, did not inhibit faith in the deliverance that God planned and continued to work for. Delayed liberation seemed to inspire a deeper faith. It seemed that suffering in the present was another motivation for belief in God. Without that belief, suffering would be without hope, and therefore unbearable. I felt close to this use of the Hebrew Bible as a liberating paradigm applied to life in the present. The Black church also felt foreign to me, however.

Far from the Black church was the Jewish post-Holocaust discussion of whether the efficacy of God was disproved by suffering. In the Black church the discussion of where God was in relation to slavery, as a parallel to where God was at Auschwitz, seemed absent. For Black Christians, God was distinctly present during slavery. Otherwise how would the slaves have survived their ordeal and been delivered? Though the delivery from slavery had also been waylaid for more than a hundred years, with new enslavements occurring after slavery ended, God was still with them. This was the only way a final liberation could be achieved.

Jews decided differently. For Jews, power was liberation—achieved at a distance from God. The Holocaust confronted the liberation found in the Exodus. This confrontation created an impasse from which there was no way ahead except through power. Discussions about God were fine if they didn't interfere with the new obligation of securing power. For many Jews, power had become a god.

Some years later, I went to Maryknoll to teach at the

school of theology, and my involvement with Christian theologies and social commitments deepened. In liberation theology, I discovered a global yearning for liberation among diverse geographical and cultural communities. In my travels in Africa, Latin America, and Asia, I experienced this theology firsthand. I traveled to the expanding cities of each region, and I traveled extensively in rural areas. As I had in New York, Atlanta, and New Orleans, I spent most of my time among the poor.

Maryknoll, the American Catholic society that sends people on foreign missions, was founded in the early part of the twentieth century to convert pagans in China to Christianity. As the missionaries spread around the world, their overall mission focus began to change in the 1960s. By the time I arrived at Maryknoll in 1980, their outreach had changed from converting pagans to journeying with those on the margins of the societies they served. As Maryknollers changed their perspectives, they began to fight for people's basic rights as citizens and for the material justice they had been denied.

Justice work meant a change in the missionaries' understanding of conversion. The conversion of society to more justice and dignity for all might involve conversion in the traditional sense of changing from a non-Christian to a Christian. However, the more interesting and complex conversion was the transformation of unjust societies into just societies. This alternative understanding of conversion emerged in situations, for example in Latin America, where both the powerful and the oppressed claimed to be Christian. If being

Christian meant participating in the world's struggles for justice and dignity, rather than simply accepting a message of salvation and awaiting a secured afterlife, then those who oppressed others required conversion. Liberation theology called those with power to that different kind of conversion. As I traveled the world of the poor, I wondered if this could be a call for a Jewish "conversion" as well.

A changed understanding of conversion flowed from the controversial assertion of Latin American liberation theology that God is present in the struggles of the poor. Another controversial assertion follows: that God is against injustice and against those who structure society in an unjust way for their own benefit. These assertions are cast in theological language, which says that God in the Bible is with the poor and the marginalized and against injustice and wealth accumulated in unjust ways. This biblical God still stands with the world's poor and marginalized. In the struggle between the poor and the wealthy God takes sides. It is incumbent upon all Christians to do the same.

Another challenge presented itself to me. Was the biblical God that liberationist Christians claimed also my God? Had Christian liberationists reversed the pattern of inheritance, first receiving that God from Jews, and now, after our having lost that God, offering God back to us? Of course, most Jews had little knowledge of Latin American liberation theology, and the Jewish establishment figures who knew it perceived it as a threat. They couched their criticisms in the political language of anti-Semitism, as if simply by challenging the hegemony of the United States, liberation theology was ipso facto against Jewish interests. Regardless, the emerging Jewish critique of Christian liberation theology seemed more complex to me.

Whether I visited the outskirts of Lima, where massive garbage dumps provided much of life's sustenance for the population, or the slums of Nairobi, where unemployment was so high as to be the norm rather than the exception, or South Africa, where apartheid was the legal political system, I began to think that the real danger for Jews might be to bring God back into the picture.

This God might ask the same question I increasingly asked. Was I witnessing the God who was absent in the Holocaust, the silent God, reemerging and finding his own voice again? And could I somewhere down the line find my own voice within God's?

IN THE HOMES OF MARTYRS

As I experienced the Other America(s) and the global disparity between wealth and poverty, the suffering that continued after the Holocaust chastened me. This suffering was widespread, often the result of a long historical legacy of great violence. Mass death continued apace. In the 1970s, the Khmer Rouge killed over a million Cambodians. Rwanda was ahead, waiting for the 1990s. Darfur was on the horizon.

The subjugated peoples I encountered were, as Rubenstein predicted, a warning for the future. The Holocaust, with all its particularities, should be seen through wider lenses beyond the horizon of Judaism. Did that mean I should see myself, with all of my particularity, through those same lenses, the struggles of others, just like the struggling of Jews being my own? Part of the Jewish community was telling me that my own particularity trumped what I was experiencing and that the Other Nations, the Gentiles, as it were, had their own concerns and possibilities. My concern and possibility had to do with Judaism, Jews, and Israel.

Behind this narrow understanding of the Holocaust were concerns regarding Jewishness in the world and lack of support for Jews. Jews had historically been concerned for others, especially in the nineteenth and early twentieth centuries. We had plunged headlong into the justice movements of our time. Revolutionary movements from Russia to Germany were heavily populated with Jews. Later Jews participated in progressive civil rights movements of African Americans and women. Where were those justice movements when it came to us? When the chips were down, when Jews were in need, where were these others?

Was the abandonment of Jews a lingering "old" anti-Semitism, or—of greater concern—was it a new variation? If we supported the particularity of others, why increasingly didn't the world support our variation of particularity, especially with regard to the state of Israel?

There was also the question of God. Those struggling for the poor and oppressed, as well as the poor and oppressed themselves, invoked God with regularity, sometimes with familiarity. The Vatican II and liberation theologies that Catholics and I worked and traveled with both professed to be certain of God's presence. The African Americans I taught and visited at worship were also certain. This was so different from what I had experienced as a Jew that I could not help but take notice. Especially after the Holocaust, the God language of Christians amazed me. I thought it was too easy. Yet it was also the case that this ease was tried through suffering and struggle. How could a reality that was tried through suffering and struggle be too easy?

Like most Jews, I have an ambivalent relationship to Christians and Christianity. This ambivalence is thoroughly understandable given the history between us. The Christian faith was and is foreign to me, and despite the ecumenical atmosphere that has developed between us, that foreignness remains. However, encountering so many Christian examples of suffering, suffering that was horrendous and ongoing but in which God was accepted, challenged my distance from God. I began to question whether my distance from God was based on my personal reflection or on reflections inherited from others. I thought that part of the distance I felt was a principled one: where was God during the Holocaust? Could it also be a protection from certain kinds of reengagement with the world?

The dialogue of Heschel and Rubenstein came to mind. Heschel's God, like the Christian God, was too easy for me. Rubenstein's dismissal of God was too bleak. I could see that the road ahead was going to be difficult. Neither Heschel nor Rubenstein would suffice if I kept pursuing the question of Israel and the Palestinians. Would Christian theologies of presence and liberation provide a bridge toward a new Jewishness *with* God that I could embrace?

During my first years with Maryknoll, I returned to Israel, in 1984, just as the first Lebanon war was winding down. I was invited to a retreat and conference center outside of Jerusalem called Tantur. Tantur was created as an ecumenical center where Catholics and Protestants could continue the goodwill gestures and discussions that had begun during the Second Vatican Council. Tantur was to be a place of reconciliation for Christians who had been warring militarily and theologically for centuries. What better place to take up this task than the Holy Land?

The naïveté of those who designed Tantur's mission was astounding. By the 1980s, it was deeply embroiled in the Israeli-Palestinian dispute. Tantur's leadership attempted to bring Jewish and then Muslim participants into dialogue. As always in the Holy Land, every time reconciliation seemed possible, dramatic events and the daily grind of Israel's actions upset it. In the end, the constant wars, uprisings, closures, and settlement building undermined Tantur's mission. It became yet another example where state power overwhelmed a dialogue aimed toward peace and reconciliation. When I arrived there, a countryside of olive tress and rolling hills surrounded its beautiful grounds. Within a decade, Jewish settlements surrounded it, along with the infrastructure of roads and tunnels that created a "matrix of control" for Israel's expansion into the West Bank.

I was invited to Tantur to speak on the prophetic voice in the twentieth century. By that time I had published several books on the prophetic. My third book was the first of my writings on the Holocaust and the struggle to be faithful after the Holocaust. In *Faithfulness in an Age of Holocaust*, I sketched out a methodology of fidelity for Jews and Christians. Like Rubenstein, I saw the formative event of the Holocaust as a paradigm for the twentieth century. Unlike Rubenstein, I tried to chart out a response to take account of the suffering in our time. This involved a restrained religiosity in league with the commitments of those on the very margins of religious questioning. The struggle to be faithful after the Holocaust occurred within the suffering of contemporary life. *After* is relative; for most of the world after is not yet. I had yet, however, to write on Israel, and the invitation to Tantur came—at least from my perspective—out of nowhere.[10]

I wondered if the interfaith and ecumenical prophetic community that flowed from Mohandas Gandhi, Martin Buber, Albert Camus, Peter Maurin, Dorothy Day, and Martin Luther King Jr. was a tradition in the making, with each teacher's own cultural and religious particularities somehow transcended through the prophetic. I later began to refer to this as the broader tradition of faith and struggle. I began to consider whether, as a Jew, this was also my tradition. If so, did such a tradition work with my Jewishness, augmenting and broadening it, or would it eventually take priority over my Jewishness? Was I a Jew who also embraced this old/new prophetic community as an extension of my Jewishness, or was I a person within this interfaith and ecumenical prophetic community who happened to be a Jew?

My first visit to Israel had been taken on the dare of my Hebrew-school teacher. I went solo without any personal contacts. By 1984, I was more traveled. It was time to go deeper. I accepted the invitation to Tantur with the proviso that I could stay for two weeks. I sought to deepen my understanding of Israel and the Palestinians by having a base where I could make contacts among Israelis and Palestinians. I wanted to know what I thought about the situation and how, from my new angle of vision, I would approach the situation. Where I would end up I didn't know.

I was determined to meet Palestinians and travel among them. I had seen them on my first trip and observed them from a distance. I could tell that they had become outsiders in their own land, an obvious point to be sure, but what were they like as individuals and as a people? What conditions did they live in? I needed a firsthand experience. I had anxieties about this journey among Palestinians. I knew that I would be journeying away from the Jewishness inside of me. This encounter would change me.

At this time, few Jews traveled among Palestinians. I had studied Hebrew in Hebrew school, but Arabic was foreign to me. I was still a stranger in Palestinian Arab culture. The only Jews Palestinians had met were Israeli soldiers, hardly the type of meeting that encourages trust or empathy. When I met and traveled among Palestinians, the "Jew" label caught in their throats. Hardly a word in any language bothered Palestinians more or evinced more negative emotion. My Judaism was complex, and I could see that my relationship with the Jewish community would undergo strain as I explored the issue of Israel/Palestine more. Still, the word "Jew" had only a positive connotation in my mind and heart.

As a Jew, I came without weapons, drank Arabic coffee, visited their workplaces, and sat and listened in their homes, a total reversal of their usual experience of Jews. It was also a total reversal of my Jewish experience. Palestinians had a lot to say to a Jew who came to listen. Most of those I met had been driven out of Israel in 1948, and some had become refugees a second time after the 1967 war. All of them were suffering under the Israeli occupation. Should I have expected coffee and sweets without a lecture on the arrogance and perversity of Jews?

From the first moments, I knew that the Palestinian view of Jews as a brutal, conquering, occupying, and even evil people would upset me to no end. It caused me to be physically ill. Ultimately, it would impact my understanding of Jewish life. Confronting the dark side of my own history caused a deep ambivalence about my own identity. I could hardly avoid a similar ambivalence toward the Palestinians who, unrelentingly, conveyed this message to me.

Over the next weeks I traveled among Palestinians in Jerusalem, the West Bank, and Gaza. Jerusalem, of course, was a familiar name to me, though the Palestinians' side of Jerusalem, their view of the history and importance of the city for them as Palestinians and as Muslims, opened a quite different perspective. Seen through their eyes, Jerusalem was almost a different city. Cities like Ramallah and Nablus in the West Bank were previously unknown to me. They were without a Jewish presence except for occupying soldiers, and thus, completely Palestinian. Gaza City was the same.

In the refugee camps in the West Bank and Gaza, I visited the homes of Palestinians whose young sons Israeli soldiers had killed. I encountered pictures of these young men, displayed in simple frames, hung with Palestinian flags. These flags were symbols of national resistance, and Israel, therefore, outlawed them even among Palestinians. In Arabic, and sometimes in English, the word "martyr" was written on the pictures. I had grown up with the stories of ancient Jewish martyrs and those the Holocaust had added to that roster, so I couldn't help but be jarred by the faces of the murdered and the terminology used to describe them. Sitting with parents who had lost a son, sometimes two, was depressing beyond words. For the most part, the families of the martyrs were among the poorest of the poor. Their loss of a child increased their poverty. But at least in their minds, their sons had died in the great cause of a renewed and free Palestine.

Martyrs are the seeds of faith and liberation. The very designation means that they did not die in vain. But what, in fact, did they die for? Would a free Palestine, alongside a secure Israel, be worth the sacrifice? What would it take—on both sides—to get to the two-state solution? The possibility of two states looked very distant as I sat in the homes of grieving parents and looked at the pictures of their young sons, surrounded by patriotic colors.

When I ended my visit in 1984, I wondered about the future of the Palestinians. More than two decades later and many visits since, I ask the same question. There are now thousands more martyrs, a physically disabled population that outnumbers the martyrs, and a broader Palestinian population that has endured displacement and occupation for sixty years and counting. What is their future?

As much, I wondered then and wonder today about the future of the Jewish people. Have we escaped the scarring we have caused them?

The Jewish Quest for Liberation

W hat does it mean to be a Jew after the Holocaust, after this Israel, and after what Israel has done and is doing to the Palestinian people? This question is one of fidelity to Judaism itself.

Richard Rubenstein had outlined what it meant to be Jewish after the Holocaust. So it seemed. An entire generation of Jewish theologians, along with the more practical and well-placed Jewish leaders, were writing and acting within a Holocaust script that Rubenstein had offered in the 1960s and 1970s. Though quite young as identity markers go, the Holocaust was imprinted on the Jewish imagination with tremendous force. Already by the 1980s, its original subversive quality had congealed into an orthodoxy that seemed strong enough to withstand any challenge. What, then, could I say? If I could find the words, did I dare speak them?

When I returned to Maryknoll, the atmosphere of U.S. military muscle was thick on a variety of fronts. Ronald Reagan's administration was moving full throttle, returning to American cold war interventionism after its post-Vietnam lull. Maryknoll missionaries felt the consequences of this interventionism around the world. They felt it especially in

Central America, where many priests and sisters served and where lay missionaries had brought about a new family-oriented dimension to their formerly single and celibate Catholic missionary movement.

In December 1980, two Maryknoll Sisters were brutally raped and murdered in El Salvador. The Catholic archbishop of El Salvador, Oscar Romero, had been assassinated some months earlier. They, the known, joined the thousands of unknown Salvadorans who had and would be murdered with little attention in the international press. The Nicaraguan revolution, inspired partly by Christian liberation theology, was also under siege. Reagan armed and financed militia known as the Contras. The United States also influenced and armed the government of Guatemala against an insurgent peasant and indigenous uprising, and it, too, was a conflict zone.

During this season of death, I arrived at Maryknoll. My clerical and lay students served in El Salvador, Guatemala, and Nicaragua. With my students and friends in harm's way, I felt on the front lines with them. Thousands of lives were lost, and I came to understand that, as a Jew, I could not simply observe these conflicts while suspending moral judgment on similar conflicts in Israel, or, as I would later understand, its involvements in Central America. Moving in several directions at once, I began dealing with my own ignorance about the history of the state of Israel. Aspects of the information I needed had never been gathered in any systematic way. I researched diverse Jewish views on the creation of Israel. I reread the Holocaust theology I knew and discovered work previously unknown to me.

Jane Hunter, a dissident Jew, cataloged Israel's involvement in arms dealing around the world in the pages of her periodical, *Israeli Foreign Affairs*. She noted that Central America had recently become a particularly lucrative hot spot for arms dealing. The Israeli arms industry was extensive. One Israeli author was prompted to see that industry as part of Israel's "global reach." As Hunter reported, Israel had become one of the major arms dealers in the world. Like other arms dealers, Israel sold those arms and other "security" training and materials to governments that were among the most serious human rights abusers in the world. With U.S. churches and Congress watchdogging America's involvement in Central America, the Reagan administration was struggling to maintain funding for its Contra war. Israel stepped into the breach.[1]

The assertion of Jewish innocence in the Holocaust and also in Israel had to be challenged, especially because few Jews knew of the Israeli arms industry or its role in supporting repressive and murderous governments. From the Israeli perspective, the Palestinians and the Middle East could be seen both as an extension of domestic policy and as a foreign policy intimately connected to domestic security. Dealing arms to parties unrelated to the conflict was a different story.

I digested this information about contemporary Israel as a Jew well versed in Holocaust theology and as a Maryknoll teacher deeply connected to Central America. I began to understand that the fates of the martyrs I visited in Palestine were multiplied around the world. While it is true that on the international scene Jews and Israel did not have sole responsibility for the deaths Israeli arms inflicted, Jews and Israel were not innocent either. Global arms dealing generated money and jobs in Israel's domestic arms industry, and it was an aspect of Israel's foreign trade. Israel was making a strategic gamble that the oppressive governments Israel armed would survive and support Israel at the United Nations and other international forums. Why did Jews and Israel want to be strategic allies of such despotic governments? I learned Israel also had security and armament relationships with the apartheid South African government. I found Israel's pattern of strategic alliances unbearable.

Holocaust theologians were silent on Israel's alliances, as was the Jewish establishment. Without ever mentioning the particulars, Holocaust theology implicitly sanctioned Israel's arms dealings. Rubenstein allowed for Israel to do most anything—without moral qualms—to achieve and remain empowered. I found a similar yes to Israel's self-interest in rereading Emil Fackenheim, especially lectures he delivered in 1968.

Fackenheim, a German-born Holocaust theologian, was a Jewish philosopher who had held fast to traditional Judasim, in some ways like Abraham Joshua Heschel. After the 1967 war his viewpoint changed. Fackenheim saw the sole reason for being Jewish as securing a Jewish future. Since Hitler had sought to kill all Jews, all Jews living were survivors of the Holocaust. The only place to guarantee Jewish survival was in Israel. Therefore to be faithful as a Jew was to struggle and, if it is need be, to die for the Jewish state. Fackenheim was Rubenstein's archenemy because, unlike Rubenstein, he felt that the Holocaust mandated a particular Jewish future. Rubenstein did not. However, they were united on Israel.

Fackenheim, like Rubenstein, saw the question of the God of history as an open wound. Since God was absent in the Holocaust, the Jewish people decided to act for itself— without God. Fackenheim saw this action in the 1967 war, where Israel's loss would have occasioned another Holocaust of Jews. Instead of waiting for aid, Jews in Israel and all over the world battled and won our survival. This overwhelming Jewish response elicited the creation of what Fackenheim called a new commandment, the 614th commandment: "The authentic Jew of today is forbidden to hand Hitler yet another, posthumous victory."[2]

When I first read that commandment under Rubenstein's tutelage, it struck me as a powerful statement. Jewish survival was crucial in and of itself. No one, anywhere, least of all Jews, should allow Hitler to triumph. I believed—and remain convinced today—that Hitler and the Nazis wanted every Jew dead. In that sense, every Jew is a survivor. The 614th commandment made sense. At stake is the meaning of rebuilding Jewish life, the meaning of a posthumous victory for Hitler, and, finally, a new understanding of authentic Jewish identity.

Judaism after the Holocaust could not mean traditional religious observance, as if the continuity of Jewish life had not been shattered by the Holocaust. Instead, Jews accepted the secular notion of rebuilding Jewish life as a moral and religious alternative. I accepted this understanding as well. Participating in the rebuilding of Jewish life was the imperative of our generation. However, Israel as the locus of this life, almost without critique, became difficult for me.

My questions began to coalesce around the theme of liberation. Christian theologians were raising the question of liberation from the side of the poor and the marginalized. Could it also be raised from the side of those who had once been the have-nots and now were the haves?

When I broached the subject of my writing liberation theology to a Christian theologian of some note, he responded that this was a Christian theological category. I found that many Jews thought this as well. In reading theologies of liberation I noticed that Christians were returning to the Judaic understanding of liberation in order to set Jesus free of the Christian tradition's ownership of Jesus. The Jesus of traditional Christian theology and the churches was everything but a liberator. Setting Jesus free meant returning Jesus to his original prophetic fold and understanding him in light of the Exodus. If anything, Christian liberation theology was Christianity re-Judaized. I wondered how categories had become so mixed up and, too often, mishandled.

The real question was less whether this or that theology was Jewish or Christian. What we needed was an exploration of Jewish life to see where Jews stood in relation to our tradition and the contemporary world. The question, however framed, was once again what it meant to be faithful as a Jew now. If indeed we could project what an authentic Jew after the Holocaust was, could it be a Jew who struggled with Jewishness in the world after Auschwitz and after Israel? Knowing what I knew about Israel's involvement in arms dealing, how could I say nothing?

My initial forays into a Jewish theology of liberation were moderate, but a logical next step. Our situation as Jews had changed radically over the 1970s and 1980s; the formative events of the Holocaust and Israel, though recent, told us less and less about where we were now—at least in the way we perceived both. Israel now augmented the expulsion of the Palestinians in the creation of a Jewish state in 1948 with further expulsions, settlements, military occupation, and war. While Jews had once been weak and helpless, our theology was telling us that we were still. The fact was just the opposite. We had become empowered—a third formative event in our time—though we failed to understand this reality.

We argued our weakness when we had power. Our sense of weakness was a response to the trauma of history. Despite our age of mass communication, historical events, especially when they are traumatic, affect our consciousness only slowly. This lag was psychological, but increasingly over the years, it became strategic. If we owned up to our newfound power, we would have to be accountable for and to it. We would also have to relinquish the Holocaust as the backdrop to everything Jewish.

Power that eclipses suffering and causes suffering to others loses its right to argue that its roots are in suffering. Israeli power, enabled by the Jewish establishment in the United

States, was losing its right to Holocaust speech. No doubt, the very thought of this loss sent a shudder down almost every Jewish spine. We had defined ourselves within the Holocaust paradigm; what voice would we have if we forfeited this because of our actions? Or even worse, what would happen if Jews, pondering our power, decided that Jews were also now *after* Israel. What if those Jews who came to believe this *after* spoke for more Jews than the power establishment would ever admit to? Articulating this *after* Israel was defined as heresy. Adopting the 614th commandment and finding it wanting, where else could we turn?

Perhaps we needed another commandment, the 615th commandment: "Thou shalt not demean the Palestinian people." Though I would formulate that exact commandment in the years ahead, it was implicit in those early years as I sought to create a Jewish theology of liberation. In that theology, I understood that the history of Jewish suffering was real; we did need empowerment. The creation of Israel as a Jewish state was a fact, perhaps even necessary, though, ironically, I would debate this increasingly in the years to come. In the mid- and late 1980s, however, when I was first writing on this subject, I kept a moderate tone and did not even raise the question of the 1948 war. The question was whether Israel and the Jewish establishment were pursuing a moderate course or an extreme one, a choice I couched in terms of righteousness and moderation.[3]

From the Palestinian perspective, Israel was neither righteous nor moderate. Palestinians turned the security argument for Jews and Israel upside down. Who was insecure, losing land and livelihood, occupied on a daily basis? Who had settlements built on its land where only the population of the occupier could live? Who had the strong military and the support of a major superpower? Where Jews saw weakness, others saw power. Where Jews saw the lessons of the Holocaust being carried out in terms of survival and flourishing despite Hitler, Palestinians felt that Jews themselves violated the lessons of the Holocaust.

Palestinians understood the reversal of power in Israel, as did, increasingly, their supporters. I also began to see this reversal, as did some other Jews, most of whom I knew only from a distance. I found that almost the entire history of Jewish dissent toward the use of the Holocaust and Israel was invisible or out of sight. I began to suspect that dissent had deliberately been buried.

I juxtaposed the Jewish experience of the Holocaust as a "shattered witness" with Israel as the "cost of empowerment." The shattered witness was Holocaust theologians trying to keep the history of Jews from coming to an end; Fackenheim's 614th commandment posited the reason for continuing: no more victories for the Nazis. This resonated with Rubenstein's sense that power alone was enough. By the time Fackenheim issued his commandment, however, Hitler's victory had already been denied. Jews had survived and were flourishing in America and Israel.

Did Jews still have something to contribute to the world beyond denying Hitler his victory? What was the reason to be Jewish beyond this seemingly negative proposition? The costs of the power needed to survive were as yet unaccounted for. Could they be counted if only Fackenheim's commandment was in place?

Jewish renewal movements were already challenging Fackenheim's commandment. Among them was New Jewish Agenda, a small, marginal group that asked whether unbridled power would be enough to secure Jewish survival and whether that survival without an ethical resurgence was enough to justify Jewish life in the present. I also found Arthur Waskow and Michael Lerner, progressive Jews, who sought a rebirth of Jewish spirituality, sometimes akin to New Age spirituality. Both Waskow and Lerner had been active in the 1960s in secular politics. In the late 1960s and early 1970s, they returned to Judaism while maintaining their political sensibilities.

These progressive Jews challenged the Jewish establishment for being attached to power and money and often lacking an ethical compass. In their view, the Jewish establishment was out of touch with ordinary Jews and moral aspects of the Jewish tradition. They counseled a return to Judaism within a profound engagement in the world. Jewish life in the world could continue the arc of Jewish progressive politics, and this, too, was a way of ensuring that the Nazis did not have the final word. After all, if we survived and lost our cutting-edge ethics, wouldn't Hitler have won anyway?

THE OUTER LIMITS OF JEWISH DISSENT

As I began to write, I also traveled and spoke on these moral questions. Sometimes local communities working under the

New Jewish Agenda banner hosted me. Having found Jewish institutional life barren and unwelcoming, these Jews were clearly marginal to mainstream Jewish life. In these small Jewish outposts, they tried to hold on to Jewish values they saw as missing in the mainstream community. Yet they lacked any institutional base for organizing their movement or passing it down, and their longevity was in question. The Jewish establishment was bound to notice their critique of how the Holocaust was being used and their challenge to the assertion of Israel right or wrong. I reported on their stances and the opposition they were facing.

In New Jewish Agenda's newsletter they discussed movement struggles that were common among Jewish dissenters. What relationship should Jewish dissent have to the established Jewish community? Should New Jewish Agenda members become active in mainstream synagogue life or should they abandon it completely? Should the movement appeal to institutions that had grown up around the support of Israel, ones that raised money for Israel and lobbied on its behalf, or form alternative institutions with different aims and values? The dissidents had difficulty finding the appropriate stance with regard to Jerusalem and the conclusion of the peace process. Should New Jewish Agenda argue for a separation of Jerusalem in two parts, one part as capital of the Jewish state, the other as capital of an emerging Palestinian state? They debated whether or not the two-state solution was possible or if there should be a discussion of 1948, the founding of Israel, and the expulsion of the Palestinians.

New Jewish Agenda, like later dissenting groups, decided to limit itself to the post-1967 occupation and settlements of Palestinian land in the West Bank. An extremely controversial issue was whether or not United States military aid to Israel should be conditioned on Israel ending the occupation. Many of the political movements of the 1970s and 1980s were confronting American foreign policy as a negative force of interventionism and control in the world. The question of whether Jews should ask the United States Congress to restrict aid to Israel, or make it contingent on Israel's accepting justice for the Palestinians, was in the air. Perhaps unknowingly progressive Jews fell into a trap in which they remain; unbeknownst to them—and to me—they argued for a solution that was already obsolete. A Jewish understanding of the Palestinians and their movements was also in the air and similarly controversial. If Jews needed to clean house and confront our misuse of power, did Palestinians have a similar obligation?

If dissenting Jews admitted that Israelis had done wrong, Palestinians had to admit the same. If Palestinians admitted their own sins, it would be easier for Jews to do the same. Then the equation could be changed into two rights: Israel had a right to exist and so did Palestine. However, this equation begged the question of whether there was an equality of wrongs, and the Jewish establishment would not countenance a Jewish confession. Though seemingly evenhanded, the equation of two sins and two rights clearly distorted the historic reality and the existing unbalanced power equation. In creating the state, Jews were the aggressor. With regard to the Palestinians, Israel held a monopoly of power.

New Jewish Agenda decided that discussion of the formation of Israel was off the table. In the first place, they knew little about this formation and had difficulty making judgments about it. In the second place, their engaging the mainstream Jewish community made such a discussion impossible. They had already entered a forbidden area to raise the possibility that some Israeli policies with regard to the Palestinians were wrong.

If New Jewish Agenda or any other group was to make a strategic foray into the mainstream Jewish community, blame for the Israeli-Palestinian crisis had to be spread around. Since the mainstream Jewish community saw the Palestinians as wrong for resisting the creation and survival of Israel, Palestinians were to blame for the impasses that Israel found itself in. Israel was innocent. Israel lacked a partner for peace. The Palestinians might be capable of such a peace but only after an apology to Israel and a massive change in outlook and character. If the mainstream Jewish community found some kind of balance of wrongs between Israel and the Palestinians to be inherently impossible, how could Jewish dissidents hope to raise the issue without placing at least equal blame on the Palestinians?

Soon New Jewish Agenda was outmaneuvered by a well-financed and creative magazine and movement called *Tikkun*. The brainchild of Michael Lerner, *Tikkun*, taken from *tikkun o'lam*, meaning "to restore and repair the world," began in 1986. It became the national symbol of Jewish dissent. At first *Tikkun* billed itself as the counterpart of the influential magazine *Commentary*. Founded in 1945,

Commentary began as a progressive journal of Jewish commentary on the world. Over the years, the editorial direction of the magazine had moved considerably to the right. By the 1980s it was the showcase for American neoconservative thought, Jewish and otherwise. *Tikkun* sought to counter *Commentary* as the voice of Jewish intellectuals and activists.

Some Holocaust theologians also wondered if Jewish thought had moved too far to the right. Indeed, on the original board of *Tikkun* was none other than Elie Wiesel, a big name to land for a new magazine. However, after seeing the critique of Israel in its first issue, Wiesel quickly and unequivocally resigned his board position. Speaking critically of Israel was too much for Wiesel. Was Wiesel afraid of finding his own voice of dissent, and did he fear being pushed off his Holocaust pedestal? Progressive Jews were on their own.

The energy of New Jewish Agenda and *Tikkun* and their balancing act of Jewish dissent were interesting. Both groups sought to become the next Jewish establishment. Of necessity they had to prove their "authenticity" credentials to the 614th commandment—they had to redefine what Hitler's victory meant and how best to deny that victory. To engage the discussion from that vantage point, however, they began with their affirmation of a strong Israel and an Israel that, while it should be ethical, was first and foremost in the Jewish heart regardless. But since Holocaust theology posited Israel as innocent in its creation and empowerment, Israel's flaws had to be disguised or argued away.

These Jewish dissenters contended that Israel's failings were forced upon it by a backward and unethical Arab people. Perhaps they felt this stance was needed. Jews in the mainstream could not understand the possibility of Arabs thinking ethically, having rights of their own independent of Jews, or even a politics of compromise to serve their own self-interest. Jewish dissenters had a choice: cater to the prevailing Jewish view of Palestinians and Arabs and criticize Israel around the edges of Palestinian recalcitrance, the easy road; or present Palestinians as having legitimate grievances, limitations, and possibilities, the hard road. Progressive Jews chose the easy road too often.

Were Jewish dissenters actually so different in their view of Palestinians from the Jewish establishment they ostensibly fought? Or were Jewish dissenters only being strategic in their arguments? Did they believe what the Jewish establishment promulgated about Palestinians and Arabs?

Was I guilty of this myself? As I read the New Jewish Agenda newsletter and the much glossier *Tikkun*, I felt a thinness of argumentation and, to be honest, a self-righteousness in the assertion of Jewish ethics as the primary and unique guide for Jews in the world. Regaining our ethical compass was essential for our own mission in the world. Other peoples, communities, and religions paled in comparison; the Palestinian people were way down the list in any Jewish calculation. In fact, whatever our failings, we, as Jews, knew better. Therefore, we had to take the upper hand. As we regained our inherent ethical edge, others would respond. Increasingly over the years, the logic seemed to be more and more about ourselves. The suffering Palestinians increasingly seemed only a backdrop to the more important

Jewish drama. Thus the increasingly enervating discussion continued.

Contemporary Jewish life had hit a dead end. By beginning with the Holocaust narrative, both Jewish dissenters and establishment groups, seemingly so disparate, were trapped in assumptions of Jewish exceptionalism that emphasized innocence and waywardness. They argued the middles instead of the ends. Jewish thought and action seemed caught in a time warp of its own making. American Jewish dissent existed within the Holocaust framework, and the Holocaust had become Americanized. Though it was European in origin and experience, a strange transference had taken place in its aftermath. After the Holocaust, our community leaders identified white and American as the way to secure our future. Israel defined itself as a Western nation, more at home in Europe and America than in its actual geographical setting in the Middle East. With this alliance, the Jewish world was shrinking. Jews were becoming more and more isolated from the rest of the world. Some began to think of Israel as America's fifty-first state. What were the long-range consequences of such thought?

Everything outside of us was a challenge to our survival that had to be negotiated from strength. Rarely if ever could the Palestinian others be given their own place in the world, as significant for them as our place was for us. The drama was a Jewish one, and everyone else was a sidelight. Even if we transgressed against Palestinians, their grievances had to be seen in the light of our innocence. Our history was out of balance. How would we right it? Righting it for ourselves, did we have any responsibility beyond that? Or did our responsibility begin and end with our drama, our narrative, our history?

In the view of American Jewish dissent, Israel was a surrogate for the innocence of Judaism, only gone temporarily wrong, and separation from the Palestinians was the answer. We had expelled them and conquered their land, so the end of occupation in the West Bank and Gaza might suffice for our responsibility and restore our singular purity and innocence. The idea of the Palestinian other polluting Jews is as old as Israel, the people. It seemed that both the mainstream and the dissenters of Jewish life held fast to this idea. I doubted that Jews could move forward with that understanding until we thought through the possible abatement of our fear of the other. Since that fear was so long standing, to dilute Jewish particularity might, in the end, mean that there would be no identifiable Jewishness left to lose or reform.

The Commanding Voice of Auschwitz was an unappeasable master. As years passed and generations became more distant from the event itself, however, it seemed inevitable that the Holocaust would recede in Jewish consciousness. Then, the voice of Sinai might reappear. If the voice of Sinai did not reappear, there would be little left of Judaism and Jewish life.

Power seduces the best of traditions; Judaism and Jews had not escaped that seduction. Progressive Jews had not escaped that seduction either. A militant Jewishness, masked by claims of innocence, had arrived on the scene. It would not quickly disappear. The New Age quality of Jewish renewal did not strike me as an adequate long-term response to

the crisis facing us. I began looking back in history and outside of the American Jewish community for a counterbalance
to the power of the Jewish establishment mainstream and
the insubstantial quality of Jewish dissent. I wanted a richer
timbre for my own voice.

The first and closest resources at hand were emerging
liberation movements. They offered a different kind of
Christianity. They were not interested in Christian renewal,
but in forming revolutionary Christians unknown since the
earliest eras of Christianity. Among these liberation theologies was Black liberation theology, pioneered by James Cone
and other African American theologians. Their Black freedom struggle confronted entrenched racism and liberal pan-
dering. Black liberation theology wanted neither of these.
Cone argued for a clear demarcation. Christianity had to
cease being identified as white. Jesus, too, had to cease being
white. The case for God could be made only when Christians
chose to side with Blacks in their struggle for freedom. Cone
also noted that Rubenstein's loss of God's presence, if it could
apply to any people, would seem to apply to African Americans. Noting Rubenstein's questions about God, Cone continued to affirm a living God who called Blacks out of their
present misery.[4]

Gustavo Gutierrez, the Peruvian pioneer of Latin American liberation theology, also raised the question of God in his
book *On Job*. In *A Theology of Liberation*, Gutierrez had located God among the poor masses of Latin Americans. Citing the Exodus God who takes sides, Gutierrez traced the

commitment of God to the poor through the ages. The Israelites were first, but that was because they were then on
the margins of Egyptian society. Any people on the margins
were special in God's eyes, rather than any particular identity
group. As a God of the poor, God was available, intervening
in history and clearing the path for God's chosen.

To be explained was why, if God had chosen the poor,
they, in the main, remained poor. With other liberation theologians, Gutierrez believed that suffering was redemptive
but only if the goal was its alleviation. That goal had to be
achievable, a tenet directly related to the understanding of a
liberating God. Because of this understanding of God, the
unrelenting continuation of poverty seemed a stunning contradiction of this promise of liberation. This contradiction
was also central to Holocaust theology. Along with other Jewish Holocaust theologians, Fackenheim was willing to confront God with the Commanding Voice of Auschwitz to
challenge divine inadequacy in fulfilling the promises God
had made to the people. Yet the Commanding Voice of
Auschwitz led to a dead end of power for power's sake. It also
allowed Jewish participation in global systems that exacerbated poverty and clearly divided the First World from the
Third World.

Jews benefited from systems that made poverty more
widespread. Therefore, our wealth raised for the poor the
same questions about God that Jews wrestled with. Were
Jews repeating the post-Holocaust unavailability of God by
inflicting this absence on people whom we forced to relive

the previous Jewish situation, people whom Jews now considered nonpersons? Which side were Jews on in this global struggle for justice?

Jews had hit another dead end. The way out would be found by listening to those who were struggling in the present, who could advise us of the limitations of our struggle today. We would be cautioned about our participation in the economic and political division of the world. At the same time, we could listen to the workings of other theologies dealing with oppression and liberation.

Jews could identify with Gutierrez's reflection on Job. Through Job, Gutierrez pondered the suffering of the innocent in history and God's responsibility in the alleviation of that suffering. A perennial problem to be sure, but Gutierrez, who struggles with the poor of today, perceived a situation that, despite the commitments of liberation theologians and activists, was growing worse. The Holocaust dead might haunt the world. Latin America was still being filled with dead. Some died accompanying the poor in their struggle for liberation. Had God abandoned the poor and their accompaniers?

In juxtaposing Holocaust theology and theologies of liberation, I saw the confluence of questions about God and moral commitment. Certainly the question of God's absence in Holocaust theology was real, but Gutierrez's God, who held a mystery that did not conform to our worldview, had something to say to Jews. In addition, the multiplying dead advised Jews that the killing had continued and that, in our empowerment and affluence, we could not pretend innocence.

Whatever our views of ourselves, Jews exist in and are of the world. As we trumpeted our participation in the civil rights movement, the Jewish community was drifting further and further from that commitment and its principles of justice. Latin Americans experienced a global economic system that benefited an elite in their countries and around the world. Part of this elite was Jewish. Even as Jews spoke of Jewish suffering, our affluence meant that others were suffering. The speech of Jewish suffering and innocence had to be tempered, even beyond the question of Palestinians to a consideration of the poor elsewhere, such as in Latin America. Linking with these many movements of liberation could provide us with an avenue for commitment to others and help us take stock of where we had arrived. Outside of the Middle East, the global situation revealed how dated was the Jewish rhetoric of what had been done to us.

Liberation theologies held out the possibility of broadening the Jewish view of the world. The Holocaust had condensed the majority of the Jewish population to parts of Europe, America, and Israel. Our ascendancy to political and economic power further shrank our vision of the world. This might not be helped, but our empowerment isolated us from our own diverse Jewish history. It also cut us off from entire areas of the globe.

Young Jews, especially, increasingly experienced only parts of America and Israel. Both America and Israel had populations on the margins, some of them also Jewish. Many Jews from North Africa and Arab lands were treated as less than fully Jewish upon their arrival in Israel. Non-European Jews existed on the margins of Israel's European sensibility and economy. To become fully Jewish they had to become fully Westernized—another part of the Europeanization and Americanization of Judaism. The Palestinians, now so important to Jewish history, were also Arabs. How could we come to understand Jewish and non-Jewish Arabs in a positive way if we simply adopted the prejudices of the West?

CONFRONTING THE HOLOCAUST AND STATE ZIONISM

Martin Buber was one of the most important and noted Jewish thinkers of the twentieth century. Buber was an Austrian Jew from Vienna who fled Germany during the Nazi period. Unlike Abraham Joshua Heschel, Buber went to Jerusalem in 1938 and lived there the rest of his life. Buber's seminal work was *I and Thou*, which he published in 1923. One of the most influential books of the twentieth century, it deftly combined Hasidic theology and Eastern philosophy with a potent communal spirituality and socialist bent. Buber saw spirituality as the essence of community and encounter as the foundation for Jewish renewal. Encounter was grounded in the hallowing of the everyday and the continual attention we paid to the Thou of each person, nature, and God.

Buber understood the world as divided into two parts, It and Thou, each existing within the other. "It" was the material world, viewed and used almost exclusively as an object that we needed to live physically. The "It" world could also be viewed as the "Thou" world, with our perspective changing from the objective to the subjective. Buber's famous example was a tree, objectified for the useful products that came from it or viewed for its strength, beauty, and life. Sometimes we needed the tree to sustain our physical life. However, if we saw the tree only in its "useful" capacity, we would miss the magnificence of the tree and a deeper spiritual life.

Buber felt the world had been traveling toward the It-ification of life for so long and with so much intensity that the Thou of life was threatened with extinction. The whole world was suffering from this malady, plunging headlong into one catastrophe after another. The Jewish community suffered the same myopic sensibility regarding the world. Along with others, Jews needed to think again about the meaning and purpose of life.

Buber's thought, even in its earliest formative period, was an extended meditation on the prophetic in our time, but as the years passed, he concentrated more specifically on Jewish themes, including the Hebrew Bible. Like Heschel, though with a somewhat different emphasis, Buber proposed a Jewish spiritual renewal rooted in community. A life-long Zionist, Buber argued for a Jewish homeland in Palestine, alongside the Arabs. However, Buber was opposed to the creation of a Jewish state—he was a Zionist of a special kind who believed that Jews should live in the Holy Land without a Jewish state to define that presence. We needed a permanent home in our own land, the land where we had be-

come a people, not become a nation. This land would help
Jews reroot our fragmented Diaspora life, so recently devas-
tated in the Holocaust. A Jewish presence in Palestine was
essential to this renewal, and such renewal would evolve
from the presence in the land.[5]

Buber's philosophical and religious ideas became known
around the world. His specific guidelines for the Jewish
homeland were largely unknown. I discovered that Buber
opened a broader understanding of a Jewish tradition of dissent as wide and deep as it was unknown. Ironically, following the most Jewish aspects of Buber's thought would require
me to cross a line that would separate me from large parts of
the Jewish community, first in relation to the Holocaust, then
in relation to Zionism and the state of Israel. Though the tradition of Jewish dissent spanned the twentieth century and
continued to the present, dissent by its nature is a minority
view. However much dissent makes sense, the trajectory of
Jewish life toward power with the pretense of innocence
continues. Dissenters remain on the margins.

The Jewish establishment uses the Holocaust to quash
dissent. Nothing in Elie Wiesel's early writing pointed to how
the Holocaust and Jewish suffering would come to be used.
Few Jews or non-Jews wanted to hear or read about the experience of the Holocaust, let alone deal with Jewish survivors. As Wiesel recounts, just years after *Night* was widely
read some Jews remained ashamed of the Holocaust. If Jews
spoke about the horror, they preferred to do so without the
victims being present. The more the Holocaust was invoked,

the less authority it garnered. Wiesel, along with others, such as the writer Phillip Lopate, worried about the trivialization of the Holocaust. Others claimed that their suffering was like the Holocaust, akin to it or worse. There seemed to be no end to the use of the Holocaust, and no way to decide who could use it and who could not.

Wiesel, of course, parlayed his writing about the Holocaust into a career of honors. In his meteoric rise in status, I saw the Holocaust changing into what he feared. In the end, Wiesel wanted the Holocaust guarded for Jewish self-interest but helped transform the meaning of the event into something that would inevitably be trivialized. Perhaps this was unavoidable when the Holocaust went public. Lopate wrote boldly of this in "Resistance to the Holocaust." As the use of the term "Holocaust" became more commonplace in the 1960s and beyond, Lopate found it to have a self-important, almost vulgar, tone:

> Then, too, one instantly saw the term was part of a polemic and that it sounded more comfortable in certain speakers' mouths than in others; the Holocaustians used it like a club to smash back their opponents. In my own mind I continue to distinguish, ever so slightly, between the disaster visited on the Jews and the "Holocaust." Sometimes it almost seems that the Holocaust is a corporation headed by Elie Wiesel, who defends his patent with articles in the Arts and Leisure section of the Sunday *Times*.

This patent on the Holocaust almost invoked God to silence challenges to thought and speech, Lopate continued:

> The Hitler/Holocaust analogy dead-ends all intelligent discourse by intruding a stridently shrill note that forces the mind to withdraw. To challenge the demagogic minefield of pure self-righteousness from an iconic distance almost ensures being misunderstood. The image of the Holocaust is too overbearing, too hot to tolerate distinctions. In its life as a rhetorical figure, the Holocaust is a bully.[6]

The Holocaust as a bully can become the Holocaust as kitsch, an idea advanced by the Israeli philosopher Avishai Margalit. In his essay "The Kitsch of Israel," Margalit cites kitsch as the easy identification of the represented object where the emotion evoked in the spectator comes mainly from a reference to the object. Kitsch can also become politicized and, in Margalit's terms, part of a state ideology whose "emblem is total innocence." This kitschification has happened to the Holocaust and Israel with dire consequences for the Palestinians. If Jews believe we are innocent and the Jewish mind endlessly replays images of Israeli soldiers conquering Jerusalem and Jewish men praying at the Western Wall, Palestinians can only be seen as evildoers plotting the destruction of the innocent. This Jewish mental replaying has the effect of mixing political grievances in the present time with historical images of destruction, thus the making the subjugated Palestinians into new Nazis.[7]

In discussing the Children's Room at the Yad VaShem Holocaust memorial in Jerusalem, Margalit argued that the real significance of the Children's Room is not in its

> commemoration of the single most horrific event in the history of humankind—the systematic murder of two million children, Jewish and Gypsies, for being what they were and not for anything they had done. The Children's Room, rather, is meant to deliver a message to the visiting foreign statesman, who is rushed to Yad VaShem even before he has had time to leave off his luggage at his hotel, that all of us here in Israel are these children and that Hitler-Arafat is after us.[8]

This message is also for internal consumption. For Margalit, talking of the Palestinians in the same tone as one talks of Auschwitz is an important element in "turning the Holocaust into kitsch."[9]

As I found, essay by essay, this literature on the Holocaust, an entire field began to open up, what might be called a literature confronting the Holocaust. It sought to safeguard the trauma of the Holocaust experience itself by dissecting the way the Holocaust was being used. Increasing numbers of Jewish writers in the United States and Israel were writing about this topic to untangle Jewish discourse. Though secular Jewish thinkers offered most of this confrontation of the Holocaust, the range of criticism was impressive, and theological categories were in abundance. When the critics of

Holocaust theology were confronted and often silenced by Holocaust imagery, they asserted that the Holocaust was functioning as God, sanctioning certain speech and disciplining other forms of speech. But where did this God dwell and who gave it authority? they asked. The very assumption and use of this Godly power reduced the terror of the Holocaust by its invocation as a tool of power.

In a community where God was in question, the Holocaust was not going to reign as a substitute God. Intuitively and strategically, the Jewish thinkers of a literature confronting the Holocaust went about dismantling the power that used suffering as a blunt instrument to reduce the Holocaust. They also recognized that the projection of the Holocaust as God rendered Israel as God as well.

Jews required distance from the Holocaust as a packaged commodity to gain some distance from Israel as a similarly packaged commodity. For many of these thinkers, including some Israelis, the Holocaust and Israel were becoming abstractions. The blood, fears, lives, and possibilities involved in both events were being submerged in a Jewish search for meaningful images. Were the Holocaust and Israel becoming kitsch images more important than life?

Israel wasn't born out of whole cloth. Zionism, the movement that began in the late nineteenth century and early twentieth century, saw the Land of Israel as the original birthplace of the Jewish people, to which Jews should return, but it was complicated from its very start. This movement developed because some Jewish thinkers in Europe, especially those living in the Pale of Settlement, thought that the future of Jews in Europe was in danger. None of these Zionists fore-saw the Holocaust. However, they saw that demographic, cultural, and religious forces that were strengthening the na-tion-state, and intensifying the difficulty minorities were having within the new European order, would have dire con-sequences for Jews. Though the Jewish condition in Europe was mixed and would continue to be so well into the Nazi pe-riod, Zionist thinkers were profoundly ambivalent about the future of Jews in Europe.

Writings by these thinkers, collected in a volume titled *The Zionist Idea* and edited by Rabbi Arthur Hertzberg, were eye opening. Hertzberg wanted a Jewish state that embodied the values of Judaism. He was another Eastern European Jew and a friend of Elie Wiesel. Though they agreed on the need for a Jewish state, Hertzberg published an open letter to Wiesel in the *New York Review of Books* during the first Palestinian uprising. The letter criticized Wiesel's silence on an Israel gone awry. By the late 1980s the question was what responsibility Jews outside of Israel had for Israel itself. Wiesel was usually silent, and when he did speak, it was, ac-cording to Hertzberg, in platitudes and without effect. Hertzberg wanted direct talk that confronted Israel's intran-sigence with regard to the Palestinians before it was too late and Israel crossed a Rubicon of sorts. For Hertzberg, crossing that Rubicon was the betrayal of Jewish values to such an ex-tent that the Jewish state might cease to be Jewish.[10]

In many ways the predictions of early Zionist thinkers came true: there was no future for Europe's Jews. After the Holocaust, there could be no doubt about their prescience.

When reading early Zionist essays, one wants to scream to Jews to get out of Europe while they still have time. The problem with their accuracy, however, was that every comment on the dismal years ahead seemed almost foreordained.

History is more complicated than hindsight read as foresight. The road to the Holocaust was not predestined. While it is true that Europe's Jews were eliminated, early Zionist thinkers were simply trying to work through the next decades of Jewish existence. As with any people, Zionist thinkers tried to guide the community to a life better than the one they were experiencing in the present. The Zionist idea was also complicated. Though Theodor Herzl, the Austrian founder of what became known as political or state Zionism, wanted a Jewish state, it seemed that the location of that Jewish state was of little importance. In the early Zionist movement a variety of places for a Jewish state were suggested, among them Uganda. Jews needed some place of their own where they could determine their own fate and normalize their condition.

Being a subjugated minority in Europe skewed Jewish life in economic, political, and cultural ways. In terms of the dominant European cultures, Jewish existence was marginal and deviant even in the best of times. For example, because the Bible forbids usury, the Church historically forced Jews to become the bankers and moneylenders of Europe, and Jews were narrowly concentrated in other distinct professions and businesses. Magnets for hostile attention from debtors and from the host culture for simply being Jews, Jews also stood out because of their economic placement in the everyday life of society. This marginalization and hostility affected Jewish self-perception, which, in turn, further affected the host culture's perception of Jews.

Jews of the Enlightenment hoped that the special status of Jews would dissipate through the dropping of religious and cultural discrimination in society. With the opening of European society, Jews would become citizens with the same rights and responsibilities as everyone else. With citizenship Jews could assimilate. Soon the "Jewish Question," an endlessly debated question as what to do with this distinct minority, would disappear. Jews would live peacefully in Europe as ordinary citizens. While Herzl and other political Zionists did not oppose this idea, they believed assimilation was unattainable. For a variety of reasons, including ancient prejudices against Jews, the Christian nature of Europe, and Jewish sensibilities that resisted full assimilation, the vision of Jews as equal and secure Europeans did not materialize.

The French Jewish army captain Alfred Dreyfus was accused of treason in the 1890s. The so-called Dreyfus affair led to a rise of anti-Semitism in Europe. Though Dreyfus was ultimately exonerated, this reemergence of anti-Semitism within the folds of an emancipated, post-Enlightenment Europe galvanized Jews to conclude that their condition would never become "normalized" within Europe. The idea of a land outside of Europe where Jews would gather and develop a life together gained momentum.

By the turn of the twentieth century, Zionism had become a recognized and vibrant minority movement. Some were political or state Zionists. Other strands of Zionism proposed a communal gathering to enhance Jewish distinctiveness that was being lost in a hostile, secularizing Europe. There ensued an argument among Zionists as to whether or not the normalization of Jews in Europe was desirable. They debated normalization or increased distinctiveness. Those Jews who focused on distinctiveness were called homeland, cultural, or spiritual Zionists.

Buber fell into the latter category, as did Hannah Arendt, the great German Jewish philosopher. Judah Magnes, an American rabbi and the first chancellor of Hebrew University, worked with Buber in Palestine and later with Arendt in the United States. Many Zionists took this position, but they were the three most prominent Jews involved. As with views of the Holocaust, I found far more than a static and one-dimensional view of Zionism; instead, I discovered still-important arguments that opened the question of a Jewish future.[11]

Originally, a majority of Reform and Orthodox communities had been non-Zionist or anti-Zionist. Though Israeli policy had come under increasing scrutiny and debate as I began developing a Jewish theology of liberation, disputes about Zionism and the creation of a Jewish state had been much more lively and expansive in the past. Looking ahead rather than back, I wondered if homeland Zionism could shed light on a possible future beyond the contemporary Jewish state.

The basic dichotomy between political and homeland Zionism revolved around normalization and the state. Homeland Zionists like Buber, Magnes, and Arendt

wanted a Jewish community that redeveloped and pioneered a distinctive Jewish contribution to the future.
Buber and Magnes, especially, wanted a just and committed Jewish community in the Land as a way of expressing
and enhancing the spiritual and ethical elements of Jewish
life. For them, the Jewish Diaspora could be more fruitful
with a thriving Jewish center in Palestine. However, both
feared that the politicization of that center as a state would
dilute and perhaps overtake the spiritual and ethical values
they wished to cultivate. Jewish ethics and spirituality
were distinctive and had existed throughout most of Jewish
history without a state. When Jews did have their state, the
results were mixed at best. Besides, a state was a state was
a state, with its own priorities and rhythms. Adding "Jewish"
before the word "state" would not change the nature of
the state. However, a state could change the nature of Judaism and mitigate the distinctive contribution a Jewish
homeland might make to Jews outside of the Land and to the
world.

Other factors affected the discussion of the Jewish community in Palestine. Palestine had become the destination
for the ingathering of Jews. The historical pull of a homeland
and the enthusiasm among Jews to move was limited, as it
turns out, to Palestine. Though Zionist propaganda saw
Palestine as the Land of Israel awaiting the Jewish return, almost as if it were empty of inhabitants, the settlers in the
early part of the twentieth century immediately experienced
the existence of another population on the soil. Regardless of
how Jewish settlers interacted and thought about them, a sig-

nificant majority of the inhabitants there were Palestinian Arabs. The Jewish settlers were a tiny, though growing, minority of the population of Palestine.

By the 1930s, Jews had become a significant part of Palestine. The challenge was how the two populations in Palestine were going to interact and the consequences of that interaction, a question for both sides as the increasing Jewish settlement movement threatened the fairly stable balance of power in the region. The debate about the configuration of Palestine was affected by World War II, the Holocaust, and a shifting global balance of power. With the establishment of a Jewish state in 1948, that discussion was over. Or so it seemed. With the creation of Israel, the question of the Jewish presence in Palestine was raised again.

Buber and Magnes saw that a Jewish state would be like any other state and diminish the Jewishness they saw as the reason for a vibrant Jewish community in Palestine. Hannah Arendt joined their opposition to Israel, adding a political reason. She thought that the creation of a Jewish state would separate Jews and Arabs within Palestine into a ceaseless war of attrition. She predicted a cycle of violence and atrocity without end because a Jewish state could be created only by expelling hundreds of thousands of Palestinian Arabs. A tremendous refugee crisis would ensue. This in turn would mean a militarization of the state, since the entire Middle East would see Israel as a foreign, even colonial, enterprise in its midst. This colonization would occur at a time when anticolonial movements were peaking in intensity. Israel swam against the historical tide. Jews would have to argue power against the turn of world history. Involved in a colonial adventure, a Jewish state would have to look west for support, again, running against the tide of Western opinion, which was reassessing its colonial past. Arendt suggested that Israel might turn into something resembling ancient Sparta.

A further danger was that a Jewish state, creating havoc in its own neighborhood, would of necessity look outside its region for superpower support to insure its existence. A Jewish state could only aspire to be a small enclave in a larger and hostile Middle East. Thus it would be forever dependent on powers outside the region. Consequently, a Jewish state would become a pawn in a larger superpower struggle, as, in its early years, it did between the United States and the Soviet Union. Since the Jewish state would be a pawn in relation to imperial powers, it would have to sell itself as a strategic asset to those powers and trim its sails to the prevailing winds. Imperial powers have their own agendas, with a Jewish state fitting that agenda for a time but perhaps not at a later date.

After the Holocaust, placing Jewish lives into such political winds was a dangerous proposition. Had Jewish leaders not learned the lessons of a politics that relied on special pleading to secure integration into a society? Being a Jewish minority had proved hazardous to Jews. Gathering a Jewish minority in a state might prove even more hazardous.

For a Jewish homeland, Arendt envisioned a new kind of politics that Jews might embody for themselves and exemplify for the world. If, indeed, Jews were a particular community with special gifts, Jews had a responsibility to share them with the world. Arendt thought that Jews could use their particularity to speak universally. Social experiments like the kibbutz and the new direction in education emanating from Hebrew University could offer an important contribution within and outside of the Jewish community. Even the revival of the Hebrew language might function in this way, an ancient language coming back into modern life. A Jewish state, needing all the resources it could garner for its survival and for its own priorities in shaping society, would, as states had elsewhere, usurp these distinctive possibilities. If the state survived at all, Jews would be transformed in service to the state. The attendant dangers of the state's survival would subvert the very reason for Jewish settlement in the Middle East.

As the Jewish state overwhelmed the homeland idea and its possibilities, it would also change internal Jewish politics around the world to reflect the needs of the state. Arendt warned that diversity of Jewish opinion and thought on this issue would be shut down. The Jewish state would increase danger for Jews and be constantly emphasized, even exaggerated, and other aspects of Jewish life would be mobilized for the state. Arendt thought it inevitable that uniformity of opinion would come to be enforced as a litmus test of Jewish "authenticity." Writing in 1948 of this threat, Arendt anticipated Emil Fackenheim's 614th commandment by two decades.[12]

Arendt predicted that the war against the Jews culminating in the Holocaust would continue after the Holocaust in the Jewish imagination. Distinctions that Jews should make with regard to this previous war, like analyzing the Holocaust in a variety of ways that included a deeper understanding of anti-Semitism as a form of racism, rather than simple un-remitting Jew-hatred, would be lost. A tautology followed: If anti-Semitism was unremitting, it was eternal; nothing could be done about anti-Semitism except to organize a state that would have the power to stop anti-Semitism at its border; all Jews outside of the state would be embroiled in a struggle against an "eternal" anti-Semitism. This notion of eternal anti-Semitism would render Jews unable to pursue the kind of political engagement crucial to Jewish survival and flourishing.

Arendt suggested seeing the post-Holocaust state of Israel's existence within the framework of pre-Holocaust European Jewry. Seen through these lenses, Jewish leaders would be unable to sift through and differentiate the pre-Holocaust and post-Holocaust political challenges to Jewry. In fact, the Palestinian Arabs and the Arabs in general have political differences, even adversarial ones, with the state of Israel. Finding comfort in the accusation that anyone who opposes the Jewish state is an anti-Semite, the state would devolve into a "Jewish authenticity" witch hunt. This witch hunt would in turn stifle Jewish thought to the point where dissenting thought might no longer be available to the community, and unanimity of opinion would be demanded. Over time, the ability of Jews to think about their future would atrophy. Arendt thought this would be a great threat to Jewish integrity and survival, as acts of aggression against Jews would intensify. Arendt begged Jews to think again.

Where Arendt saw political danger, Buber and Magnes saw spiritual disaster. They contemplated Jews and Arabs living in their own particular communities while developing bridges that encouraged political cooperation and integration. Community particularities would be focused inward and shared across community boundaries. The larger community boundaries between Jew and Arab within Palestine could eventually be shared across the broader Middle East. Buber and Magnes each proposed various confederations within the Middle East to enable all parties to exist in harmony and pursue the joint development of the region. If a Jewish state emerged at the expense of this shared political future, Buber and Magnes felt, a peaceful life for Jews and their neighbors would become impossible. For Magnes, this scenario would be fraught with so much danger on the spiritual level that it might destroy Jewry at its foundation.

Magnes's pacifist Judaism forced him to prefer the redispersion of Jews outside of the Holy Land to their concentration in a state. In 1948, as the Jewish state was coming into being, Magnes, just months before his death, personally lobbied President Truman and Secretary of State George Marshall to land troops in Jerusalem to maintain the unity of Palestine and forestall the creation of the state of Israel. Arendt predicted correctly that Magnes's lobbying against a Jewish state in the highest corridors of American power would eventually be considered heresy. Worse, it has been forgotten by most Jews or never learned at all.

As I began to find and piece together the ideas of these thinkers and activists, I discovered that Jewish dissent on Israel was indeed a tradition. I was struck that this tradition of dissent was so deeply buried that, when it was broached, many Jews accused the bearer of this tradition of lying and incitement. Speaking of opposition to the state had indeed become heresy; challenging the unanimity of thought on Israel—and the meaning of the Holocaust—meant that you were not an "authentic" Jew. Israel had become a Sparta in the Middle East, victorious for now but whose existence would also hang in the balance, and the Holocaust had become the ideological underpinnings of that Sparta. Jews around the world had become modern-day Spartans.

In 1987 (the same year my book on a Jewish theology of liberation was published), Simha Flapan, the author of *The Birth of Israel: Myths and Realities*, died in Tel Aviv. Flapan was born in Tomaszow, Poland, in 1911, and emigrated to Palestine in 1930. He had a long and distinguished career as a writer and peace activist. During his lifetime, Flapan was national secretary of Israel's MAPAM party and director of its Arab affairs department. He was founder of the Middle East monthly *New Outlook* and director of the Israeli Peace Research Institute. He also served as a visiting scholar at Harvard's Center for Middle East Studies.

I discovered Flapan's book as I contemplated the perspectives and warnings of Arendt, Buber, and Magnes. The tradition of dissent kept expanding. Flapan divided his book into seven chapters around what he called the seven myths of Israel's creation: "Zionists Accepted the UN Partition and Planned for Peace;" "Arabs Rejected the Partition and Limited War"; "Palestinians Fled Voluntarily Intending Reconquest"; "All Arab States United to Expel the Jews from Palestine"; "The Arab Invasion Made War Inevitable"; "Defenseless Israel Faced Destruction by the Arab Goliath"; "Israel Has Always Sought Peace, but No Arab Leader Has Responded." In each chapter he investigated one of these myths within its historical setting. While not rejecting every aspect of each myth or simply reversing history into another set of myths, Flapan tried to deflect the mythological aspect that has grown up around the history of the creation of Israel. His conclusion was that Israel's War for Independence and its aftermath precipitated a tragic confluence of events that led to the present impasse, which he correctly predicted would long outlive him. In Flapan's view, the Arab world held its breath and wanted to work out a settlement with the new state of Israel. Israel, for its own reasons, rejected these compromises out of hand. In defense of Israel's innocence, these myths were offered to the Jewish public and the world. Since that time Israel and Jews in general have been guided by this mythological view of the conflict.

Israelis hold these myths to be self-evident, or at least Israeli historiography held them to be so. In fact, at the time that Flapan was researching and writing his book, many Israelis knew better, since they participated in events that later became mythologized. Their knowledge, however, was overwhelmed by the state's need to create a mythological past.

Many American Jews held these myths to be self-evident then, and they still hold them very nearly as a sacred trust today. More than two decades after the publication of this book, most American Jews believe that even discussing such myths is beyond the pale. For those who do speak and write about them, there are immediate outcries to censor such speech as anti-Semitic. Flapan's myths are seen as anti-Semitic, a roster of elements used to undermine the existence of Israel. Instead of looking critically at the founding of the state, as new histories that demythologize the founding of America have done, for example, many Jews consider a critical view of Israel by one of Israeli's founders a weakness and even a threat to Jewish existence.

As important as the demythologizing of Israel's founding years was Flapan's hesitation to pursue and publish his findings. A veteran of Israel's founding war and an Israeli citizen, Flapan would seem to have been well placed to offer such a study. The opposite was the case. He had his own hesitations; friends and colleagues also counseled him either not to pursue his research or to write and publish it in a way removed from the public debate:

> Friends and colleagues with whom I have worked closely for many years advised me not to present the subject of my research as a challenge to Israel's long-held and highly potent myths. They suggested that I simply make my contribution in a non-committal academic manner, describing the evolution of the Arab-Israeli conflict and leaving the conclusion to the reader. Out of respect for their work and over many years of collaboration, I gave considerable thought to their proposal. But I concluded that such an approach would defeat the very purpose of the

book. It would have produced a very detailed historical study interesting only to historians and re-
searchers, whereas, in my opinion, what is required
is a book that will undermine the propaganda structures that have for so long obstructed the growth of
the peace forces in my country. It is not the task of
intellectuals and friends of both peoples to offer ad
hoc solutions, but to hold the roots of the conflict up
to the light of intelligent inquiry, in the hopes of
sweeping away the distortions and lies that have
hardened into sacrosanct myth.[13]

As Flapan's counselors surmised, the public airing of Israel's mythologies was just the tip of the iceberg. In the 1980s
and 1990s a group developed that the Israeli press called the
"new Israeli historians." These writers and academics deepened Flapan's understandings with more historical detail
from recently opened Israeli archives. Among the new Israeli historians were Benny Morris, Avi Shlaim, and Ilan
Pappe. They wrote intricate histories of Israel's founding
with particular attention to the creation of the Palestinian
refugee population.[14]

With some twists and turns, these historians validated
and detailed the Palestinian version of historical events,
which had been seen up till then as Palestinian and Arab
mythology. The Palestinian refugees originated with the creation of the state of Israel. Jewish soldiers, some of them recently arrived in Palestine as survivors of the Holocaust,
forced Palestinians from their home in villages, towns, and

cities and expelled them across the borders into the West Bank, Gaza, Jordan, Egypt, Syria, and Lebanon. Later, the former deputy mayor of Jerusalem Meron Benvenisti and then Haifa University historian Ilan Pappe would refer to this expulsion as ethnic cleansing. Unlike its mythology, Israel did not have a virgin birth.

ISRAEL BURNING

In 2007 I traveled to different parts of the world to celebrate the twentieth anniversary of *Toward a Jewish Theology of Liberation*. With our instant culture, a book that still has some mileage at twenty years of age is almost a miracle. Rather than being old and out of date, I felt, the message of the book was more relevant than when it was first published. This should have made me happy. It didn't. I would have been much happier to celebrate a book that was relevant in its time and helped to make the change that rendered the book irrelevant.

By 2007, many Palestinians had given up on the two-state solution. Through the occupation, Israel had taken so much land for settlements that little remained for a viable Palestinian state. Israel had ostensibly withdrawn from Gaza; at least its small number of settlers had been forcibly removed. However, Israel, with Egypt, maintained control over Gaza's borders. Palestinians and some Jewish observers likened Gaza to a vast prison camp. Its more than one million occupants were among the largest jailed populations in the world.

What to do with such a mass of incarcerated humanity? Arguments within the Israeli political system abounded, especially when the inmates became unruly and fired homemade and errant incendiary devices across the border into Israel. Since Israel controlled the electrical grids and other aspects of essential services in Gaza, as well as its borders and airspace, debates and punitive actions were tied to the understanding of Israel's own security needs. Israel punished Palestinians with denial of food and electricity. Of course, there was also the alternative of reinvading Gaza, which Israel did on a number of occasions. Meanwhile the settler population in the West Bank more than doubled in the 1990s and continued to grow during the first decade of the new century.

The Separation Wall, begun in 2000, neared completion. The use of the word "separation" could not disguise the fact that the wall marked out a permanent presence of Israel deep in the West Bank and on both sides of the resident Palestinian population there. That presence encroached on Palestinian land and separated into unequal territorial parts the Jewish and Palestinian populations in the West Bank. During this time a group of Israeli architects argued that Israel's permanent presence in Jerusalem and the West Bank was a civilian rather than a military occupation. The civilian occupation required the participation of every level of Israel's civilian, corporate, and governmental structure. How else could the massive and connecting infrastructure of Israeli towns and cities be built, developed, and maintained? The military apparatus executed its role to protect that infrastructure.[15]

Subsequently, whenever I traveled to Israel and Palestine, I passed through terribly sophisticated checkpoint terminals that Palestinians had to use as they traveled to and from Jerusalem. I went from Jerusalem to Bethlehem to speak at a conference, and I brought my son, Aaron, then twenty years old. Orders were barked out in garbled tones that made the language spoken seem from another planet. Passing through the terminal together, we viewed the wall that surrounded Bethlehem. Each of us commented on the Israeli sign on the wall, in Hebrew, Arabic, and English: "Peace Be with You!"

The Israeli settlement of the West Bank was a continuation of the Israeli settlement of what had become the state of Israel with the expulsion of the Palestinians in 1948 and later. Before the expulsion of Palestinians, Jews gathered in settlements located on the Mediterranean coast. With the sudden opening of the interior to Jewish settlement, the challenge facing the government was to promote Jewish settlement in the newly vacant land. Thus the post-1967 settlements were only the latest part of a familiar scenario. They represented a continuing westward movement of Israel and its Jewish population.

Not only does Israel lack a virgin birth, but from the beginning it has been a settler society. Another myth is the extremist fundamentalist settler Jew as the main settler population. We have heard about such Jews for decades as an ideological component of the settler movement that prevents a solution to the Israeli-Palestinian conflict. From the beginning, however, the expropriation and settlement on Palestinian land has been logical, well planned, and sanctioned by Israeli government and society.

During the decades that I researched and wrote on the subject of Jewish identity and fidelity to Judaism, my understandings of the Holocaust and Israel had shifted tremendously. This book's title is an equation, "Judaism does not equal Israel." It turns out that "The Holocaust does not equal the Holocaust." Nor does "Israel equal Israel."

Nothing is as it seems. There are multiple levels of meaning and contested understandings. Some understandings have won; others have lost and been buried. The lost and buried await exhumation and application.

Knowledge that unveils false mythology is enlightening and invigorating. Learnng more about any subject alerts one to layers left to be explored. Intellectual inquiry is exciting because with each new layer one reaches, more knowledge is available, and decisions about life, including what to do next, become more clear and available. Knowledge means options. Knowledge that unveils mythology can also challenge the identity of a community.

The more we probe identity, the more fluid and changing it becomes. Identity explorations become exciting adventures, rather than static claims. Unfortunately, this excitement is often tempered by the challenge of relating to others. What is moving and crucial to one may seem quite dangerous to another. Exploration of identity is usually not

appreciated by establishments that have their identity—
and their livelihood—attached to certain notions of self-
definition. When identity is fixed, it is also usually accompanied by a fixed view of the other. Reexamining identity also
puts definition of the other in flux. We may even discover the
other within.

Examining mythologies can become so disruptive that
those who do such examinations may censor their own conscience. In this dilemma lay the warning to Flapan; his
friends and colleagues sought to stop him from opening a
Pandora's box of thoughts about Israel's myths. Still, Flapan
did open that box. Others rushed in. The Jews that rushed in,
Israelis like Flapan, took heat from some and were admired
by others. By the time Flapan had become known for his
myth breaking, he was no longer alive. When the new Israeli
historians began writing they were in their thirties and early
forties. Life lay ahead of them.

The time frame for uncovering the myths that surround
the Holocaust and Israel is short. Since both events are relatively young, their age being measured in decades rather
than centuries, the uncovering of the foundational store is
also quite young. Thus the energy of myth creation and consolidation collides with the energy of myth unveiling and unraveling. Added to this complexity is that there is so much at
stake.

The Holocaust took place within my own father's lifetime, quite close at hand. The Holocaust and Israel have become central in my lifetime. Thoughts about Jews and Jewish
identity remain ambivalent, at least in Europe and America,

and, despite great strides forward, this ambivalence remains. My son and I view changes as they are happening. Jewish history is ancient and totally contemporary. It is happening in real time.

Some seek to dethrone the "myth" of the Holocaust for sinister means. Holocaust denial exists, and sometimes it is represented at the pinnacles of state power. One has only to think of the fulminations of the Iranian president, Mahmoud Ahmadinejad, to hear the Holocaust denial myth raised to the level of state policy. I can understand using the Holocaust as a shield and as memory, but the difference is that Jewish leadership in Israel and America has placed Jews in a contemporary bind. Jews now possess ideological and political power.

One cannot be complacent or lured into believing that the five million or so Jewish citizens of Israel are safe and secure forever. In Israel's 2006 invasion of Lebanon, Hezbollah forces were able to fire rockets into Israel. During the Lebanon war I kept a daily diary. Midway through the war I noted: "Lebanon is burning. Israel is burning." As the war progressed, it was evident that Israel was quite vulnerable to attacks that could destabilize or even destroy its society. It is surrounded by such dangers.

A scenario of escalation is not hard to imagine. Israel's nuclear arsenal is at the ready, and though its use might doom Israel itself—the distance between countries in the Middle East being so small that blowback would probably be inevitable—the scenario of Israel going down and bringing the Middle East down as its last act is hardly far-fetched.

These past years have seen Iraq and now Iran boast of their military prowess. Though big-bang revenge plots can end up as whimpers in the realities of the world, the end of Israel and the Middle East would bring on a horror beyond imagining.

What would it take for American Jews on the local or national level to speak out about Israel's nuclear arsenal, and how would Holocaust theology function if indeed Israel nuked a city the size of Beirut or Damascus or Cairo? So much has happened already that the voices of the Jewish establishment are no doubt ready for any eventuality. Still, they could not continue to speak about Jewish innocence or raise the Holocaust banner high.

Like all dissenters who speak publicly, I have experienced discrediting attempts and attacks. I can speak from experience that the arguments and explanations would be laughable if they weren't so sad. After these many years I think the most difficult part of my journey is watching Jews stoop so low in defending the indefensible. That is why I have concluded that we as Jews have reached an end in our history. The question is whether there is a way forward.

3

Can Jews Redeem Christianity?

The Holocaust happened, was horrible beyond words. Jews were targeted, singled out; Hitler didn't work a gaming table where any one group could have been singled out if the dial had just landed on them. His anti-Semitism had deep roots. Christian anti-Semitism laid the ideological and historical groundwork for the Holocaust. During the Nazi era, Christians were also culpable in their silence and relative indifference to what was happening to Jews. In the face of the Nazi onslaught, European Jews were alone.

So the equations "The Holocaust does not equal the Holocaust" and "Israel does not equal Israel" must also be taken solely for their intended meaning, lest they feed a new mythology. Jewish thought and theology are caught in a conundrum, surrounded by those on all sides who wait for the issuance of new understandings that will reinforce, reestablish, or demolish the myths that sustain so many. If this was just an academic game, saying the yeas and nays regarding postmodern interpretations of language and the self, intellectuals would be free to explore crucial questions without fear of causing destruction and bloodshed. Jews have rarely been free-floating thinkers; nor are they today.

So what are Jews to do? An entire history, the recent past, and Jewish identity for the future are at stake, and the pressure is enormous. We are warned against endangering the Jewish people, exposing us to ridicule, hypocrisy, and worse. Safety issues for Jews both inside and outside of Israel remain. So, too, does the monitoring of Jewish dissidents by the Jewish establishment. Dissenting Jews are not safe from Jewish power.

The "friends" of the Jewish community must also be called to an accounting. Usually, these friends support Jews willingly and without complaint. They support only part of the Jewish community, however. The Jewish establishment works to silence offenders who show support for dissenting Jews. Public shaming with accusations of anti-Semitism is often the weapon of choice. Jobs and other opportunities can diminish or disappear. For good behavior, there are rewards, among them access to institutional and career advancement. In the political realm, perks and punishments are handed out at will. To hold public office in the United States, friends of Jews must pass a litmus test of loyalty to Israel. The academic realm is monitored carefully. Ironically, the fields of Jewish and Holocaust studies, once scorned by many universities, now often provide the venue for the policing of Jewish dissent and its allies.

Rabbi Irving Greenberg was a major determiner of awards and punishments. He warned that the Jewish prophetic threatened what he called the third era of Jewish history. The first era was the Biblical Era, when Israel was formed and God was directly involved with the Israelite peo-

ple. The second era was the Rabbinic Era, when the rabbis
guided Jews through the Diaspora reality without the direct
voice of God. The third era, as yet unnamed, is guided by the
Holocaust and Israel. Each era had a guiding principle that
defined the work of the Jewish people. In the third era any
commentary or action seen as detrimental to the memory of
the Holocaust or the survival of Israel must be policed and
sanctioned. Any Jew who interferes with this work is to be
shunned and, formally or informally, excommunicated.

In this atmosphere of silencing dissent, the decline of
Holocaust theology is noteworthy. The last original work,
Greenberg's "The Ethics of Jewish Power," appeared in
1988. Greenberg penned it as a response to the Palestinian
uprising. In this essay he argues that Israel has to be judged
by normal standards of state behavior. He warns of the Jewish prophetic demanding more than any nation can deliver
on its highest ideals, especially Israel. Greenberg affirms that
Jews want more from Israel as a Jewish state than they expect
from other states. Other communities and states also demand too much of Israel.[1]

In this third era of Jewish history, Jews still need to affirm
the specialness of being Jewish and the specialness of Israel
as a Jewish state. At the same time, Jews, now with the necessary power to secure their existence, have to deal with the
complexity of power. This means that Jews will have to live
with Jewish power that sometimes crosses the ethical line
and also form alliances with groups, institutions, and nations
that, in the best of all worlds, Jews would not choose to align

with. Jews and Israel have permanent interests, not permanent friends. Jews have to go where the power they need is
located. Greenberg believes that Israel can only be 10 percent better than other nations and still survive. Like any nation, Israel makes its share of miscues and should admit
those mistakes and rectify them. What cannot be tolerated is
a demand that Israel be too much better than other nations.
Prophetic criticism weakens Israel. Those who ask too much
from Israel should be charged with anti-Semitism. Whether
intentional or not, this criticism lays the groundwork for another Holocaust.

Greenberg calls the political world of permanent interests "normalization," echoing a dream of state Zionism. Normalization means that Jews and Israel will act more and more
like the other nations and preserve only the 10 percent dif-
ferential. All Jews must accept normalization. The prophetic
in Jewish sensibility and life is the greatest obstacle to Jewish
survival. Greenberg accepts that as a pervasive influence
since ancient Israel, the prophetic has provided the basis for
much Jewish thought and action through the ages.

According to Greenberg, when Jews do not understand
the changed situation of Jews in the world, the prophetic
voice is applied indiscriminately, which is a grave error in
judgment. The Rabbinic Era already disciplined the prophetic. Since Jews existed as a small minority among hostile
host cultures with little room to expand, let alone dissent
against injustices inflicted upon us, the rabbis discouraged
and even persecuted prophetic movements within Judaism.

The community could ill afford Jewish prophetic movements that sought solidarity with radical political groups that undertook to confront the larger culture.

Of course, despite these prohibitions, Jewish prophetic thinkers emerged and were especially visible in the late nineteenth and early twentieth centuries. They continue to exist after the Holocaust. At first most of this prophetic thinking was geared toward the unjust structures of the non-Jewish ruling elite. Now that Jews have assumed power, in many cases we *are* that elite, or are significantly aligned with it. Often as not, this Jewish power draws the same scorn from the Jewish prophetic voice as in previous times, when Jews had little access to that power.

Greenberg argues that though power itself needs to be scrutinized, for Jews, "Jewish" before power is an important qualifier. To call for major changes when Jewish power remains insecure is tantamount to treason. Greenberg's ethics "of" Jewish power is based on this fundamental insecurity. Ethics must now be analyzed within the normalized Jewish condition. Minor adjustments in the use of power can be called for. The conduct of Israel's wars can be scrutinized, for the most part, only after the war is over. Certain questions are out of bounds—obviously, interrogation of what actually occurred in the creation of Israel is too explosive a question. Another is the unification of Jerusalem after the 1967 war. Israel's occupation as permanent and intentional also falls beyond the pale. Utterly unthinkable is the possibility of a Jewish homeland whereby a Jewish state would whither away and Jews and Palestinians would live in equality without privileging ethnic or religious identity. With all the significant issues off the table, Greenberg so limits Jewish dissent that the prophetic is hardly the issue. Simple normal political discourse is made difficult or impossible.

Greenberg fulfilled Hannah Arendt's dire predictions about the future of Jewish life. Indeed, Greenberg's essay closed the arc on the radical dimensions of early Holocaust theology. In a just a decade or so, discussion of the Holocaust moved from a subversive theology that upset the main institutions and consciousness of the community to a theology that marked out an orthodox understanding of Jewish identity.

Anxiety now lodges at the heart of that Jewish identity, especially anxiety over the prophetic. This anxiety parallels the violence that has become part and parcel of normal Jewish life. Though the violence is often seen as coming from outside, with Jews only and necessarily responding to that violence because we have no choice but to respond or perish, in fact a voluntary and self-serving violence is now intrinsic to our Jewish way of life. The fear is that without violence, Jews will disappear. Such is normalization. In the end, Jews exercise violence like others who benefit from violence. Like other communities, we leverage violence for our own sake, and like others, we claim innocence in that exercise. Still, with the prophetic disciplined but still lurking in the background of Jewish life, a profound unease pervades the community. This is why Greenberg attempts to justify historically our journey into normalization and why he rationalizes what has heretofore been unacceptable.

Greenberg does double duty as a theologian. He knows that the biblical prophets were especially active when Jews were in the Promised Land. He knows that their critique often had dire consequences for Jewish power, including the threat and actuality of being expelled from the Land completely. By removing the prophetic, he assures Jews of our ability to continue on. The prophetic is dead. No worries!

Though Holocaust theology in its decisive and original formation is part of the past, its residual effect remains as if it has been engraved on Jewish life. When the issue of Israel is raised, the Holocaust is referenced. When questions about the use of the Holocaust arise, Israel is referenced. Most of this "understood" reality is now lodged within Jewish institutional life as well. The power of modern Jewish institutions once derived from the tidal wave of Holocaust memory that Elie Wiesel and others evoked among ordinary Jews. Now these institutions have their own base of operations nearly independent of ordinary Jewish support. In the main they rely on donations from a small circle of wealthy Jewish donors. They also derive their status and support from non-Jews who support Jewish causes from their own perspective on the Holocaust.

From the beginning, the memory of the Holocaust was forged in the West, primarily in America and in a culture dominated by Christians. After the Holocaust, many Christians understood that their theological presuppositions about the singularity of Jesus and his redemptive mission had defined Jews as Christ deniers or had accused Jews of murdering the Messiah God. Christians began to understand that their own theology of salvation placed Jews at risk. The result was persecution, ghettoization, and the death of Jews. The logical conclusion of this history was the death camps. Jews came into contact with liberal Christians after the war in a new theological engagement characterized by Jewish assertion and Christian repentance.

Though the discussion among Christians with regard to Jews is long-standing, the traditional Christian understandings of Jews have been simple: Jews were God's chosen; God promised a Messiah; the Messiah came in the person of Jesus; Jews rejected and murdered him; Christians accepted the Messiah that was promised to Jews, which they rejected; Christians are the New Israel replacing the Old; the Old Israel is now condemned to wander the earth under God's punishment; Jews are witnesses to the possibility of God's love and God's punishment; at the end of time, even the Jews, blinded by their own ignorance and stubbornness, will see. The conversion of Jews will be the sign of the approaching end-time, but, in the meantime, Jews must be punished and separated from Christians lest their sly intelligence and denial permeate the Christian community and influence the righteous to disbelieve.

For Christians, Jews were the witness people. Jews witnessed in their scriptures to the coming Messiah and the truth of Christianity, which they rejected. While witnessing to the truth they rejected, Jews were also examples of what happened to holders of the promise when they denied the truth. The glory of the Jews was in the past. Hostility toward Jews became the paradigmatic attitude toward all unbelievers.[2]

The religion of the Jews, Judaism, was also part of this witness. Insofar as Judaism preserved the Torah, God's revelation of the coming Messiah, Jews had a religion worth understanding. However, since Judaism was built around the Talmud, a series of ever-evolving rabbinic commentaries on and interpretations of the Torah compiled after Jesus's death, Judaism was an invalid religion. The Talmud itself was often the object of defacement, ridicule, theft, and burning. If Judaism was a living religion alongside Christianity, then the battle of Christianity and Judaism was a living one. The ongoing reality of Judaism violated in a deep and abiding way Christianity's sense that it had replaced Judaism as the New Israel, the favored people of God.

Christianity created a profound quandary for itself. Jews were important for Christians and were reviled. Jews revealed what happens when a people disobeys God. They were witnesses, and in their chastised state, existing on the margins of Christian power, they were object lessons for Christian triumph and apostasy. Having Jews around kept alive an example of disobedience. By their very existence, however, Jews challenged the truth of Christianity. Jews as examples of defiance against God were, thus, part of Christian destiny. Ghettoized and marginalized in special occupations, Jews remained to interact with non-Jews. The pressure had to be kept on Jews, lest they become legitimate interlocutors of Christian belief. Since they were essential to the Christian imagination and a touchstone in the present, as well as being possible converts as the end-time came near, Jews could not be allowed to disappear entirely. The witness people could be persecuted; they also needed protection until the end-time.

Since the Nazis had a different end-time scenario, a world without Jews, the idea of the witness people and Jews as the eschatological reserve became passé. Jews lost their function within the Christian economy of salvation, which, though based on a negative perception of Jews, preserved their lives because of the possibility of conversion to the true religion, Christianity. The Nazis denied the possibility of Jewish conversion to the truth; once a Jew, always a Jew. Under the Third Reich, Jews, along with being a religious classification, became a race.

The Nazi classification scheme saw racial mixing as a degradation of the original and hierarchical placement of races. The Jews were the lowest classification partly because they were so insidious; Jews were the parasitic survivors of this racial system. Because of their intelligence, distorted and perverted as it was, they survived by latching onto and subverting others. For Christians, Jews were Christ killers. For the Nazis, they were parasites. Christians needed Jews alive. For the Nazis, the only good Jew was a dead one.

When Christians woke up after the Holocaust they were confronted both by their own theology of the Jews and by the distance to which Nazis had taken that theology. For many Christians, the Nazis were the antithesis of what they thought to be Christianity, a religion of truth to be sure, but also one of love and forgiveness. Yet Christianity had its own issues relating to Jews. It was only a small step from the ghettos of Christian Europe to the Nazi gas chambers.

For American Christians, the idea of ghettoizing Jews was an anachronism, foreign to the American spirit let alone to the Christianity preached in its post–World War II pulpits. Enlightened Christians, especially affluent ones or those living in large urban areas, interacted with Jews, at least in public. The segregation of Jews and Christians, though played out in social and business settings, was essentially foreign to the American spirit. Segregation was left for African Americans, and even that segregation was already in dispute in the postwar years.

The unraveling of Christian and Nazi history regarding Jews began in earnest after the Holocaust. It continues today. Christians began to examine theologies that placed Jews in a negative light and had led, and might lead yet again, to the horrors of the Holocaust. Such theologies were unseemly in the enlightened era of American triumph. Christians in America wanted nothing to do with the skeletal figures they saw looking out at them from the "liberated" death camps. Vatican II was a marker on the journey of unraveling. Under the guidance of Pope John XXIII and assisted by Jews like Abraham Joshua Heschel, the Roman Catholic Church began reformulating the Jewish-Christian argument into an extended civil conversation about covenant, God, and salvation.

A revolutionary approach to Jews and Judaism made its way into the Catholic Church and the world. Jews were freed of the charge of deicide, and the Church affirmed the continuing covenant of the Jews. Degrading ideas of Jews and Judaism were removed from the Catholic catechism and liturgy. Jews were seen as forerunners of Jesus the Christ and as being a God-fearing people in the present. Years later, Pope John Paul II visited a synagogue in Rome. He referred to Jews as "our elder brothers." With this shift, Jews serve as witness people in a positive way: the closer to Jews and Judaism Christians are, the more Christian they become. Some Christian theologians have gone so far as to say that without Jews and Judaism as co-partners, Christianity cannot exist in its own authenticity. As an extension of Judaism, Christianity requires Jewish roots alive and well in the present. Otherwise, the Christian branches wither and die.

Christians have never had a normal relationship with Jews. From the beginning, Jews played an overly determined part of Christian reality. The early debates about whether the "New" Testament trumphed what Christians called the "Old" Testament accompanied the question of whether the Jewish scriptures should be part of the Christian canon at all. When the dominant forms of Christianity decided that the Jewish scriptures were in fact essential to the testimony of the coming of Jesus the Christ, the Jewish scriptures became an interpretative breeding ground for negative images of Jews, especially when seen in light of the New Testament accounts of Jewish perfidy. The Hebrew prophets' critiques of injustice were turned into attacks on the intractability of Jews and became justification for the punishments they deserved. Christians read negative images of Judas backward and forward in the evolving Christian understanding of ancient and contemporary Jews.

That Christianity clearly came from Jews and that Jesus

himself was a Jew did not hinder Christian theologians. They argued that Judaism was corrupt at the time Jesus arrived on earth and had been corrupt ever since. True, Jesus may have been Jewish in his upbringing, religion, and culture; but he departed from his origins by placing himself against contemporary Jewish life. Since he heralded something new and beyond the Judaism of his time, Jews had him crucified. The truest marks of Jesus as the revelation of God were his separations from any Jewish identity or traditions.

Not only did *the* Jews of his time crucify Jesus, but also, from that moment on, all Jews everywhere and of every generation were likewise culpable in Jesus's death. To overcome their long anti-Jewish legacy, post-Holocaust Christians had to change their caricatures of Jews and of historic Judaism. Jews and Judaism became religious co-travelers. With this shift in defining Jews, Christians turned the unredeemable negative into an unredeemable positive. The demonization of Jews turned into their romanticization.

In Christian liberal religious circles, this idealistic, stylized aesthetic of Jews became crucial to Christian renewal. To escape association with the ceaseless Nazi slaughter of Jews and the damning portrait of two millennia of Christian anti-Semitism, Christians now romanticized Judaism. The Jews, once accused of murdering the Lord and Savior of the world, would now redeem the Christian view of salvation by being taken into the very heart of the Christian future.

As Christians emptied their language and ritual of anti-Jewish sentiments, their own sense of Jews and Judaism changed. The Jewishness of Jesus, once subject to interdiction, was now redeemed in the Christian canon. Christian scholars highlighted how Jesus was born and raised a Jew, interacted with his Jewish culture, and affirmed Jewish values of justice and compassion. The distinctiveness of Jesus remained, especially in his call for forgiveness, his special intimacy with God in calling him Father, and his willingness to suffer for God's reign on earth.

Jesus brought a salvation different from what Jews expected, and Jewish leaders' rejection of him was understandable. Besides, whatever these authorities' disputes with Jesus, only the Romans had the power to execute criminals and troublemakers. Rather than the Jewish people who followed him or Judaism in general, Jesus's disputes with religious and political authorities aligned with the Roman Empire led to his execution. The Catholic Mass after Vatican II further absolved *the* Jews from culpability in the death of Jesus, for as God had preordained Jesus's coming, suffering, and death, Jesus's Passion was also part of God's plan. The birth of Christianity, in this new Christian theology, was carried forth by Jesus's Jewish apostles. Most prominent among them was Paul, an indefatigable proselytizer, whose primary mission was now seen as to the Gentiles. Jews were a mystery to Paul. With all his thinking and writing on Jews, Paul went back and forth on the meaning of his heritage. True, Paul saw the Jews as missing the moment of salvation, but, through these new Christian interpretative lenses, that might be part of God's providence.

The overall sense of Paul was that Jews stayed in good standing till the end of time, which he thought was imminent. Soon everything would be sorted out. It seemed inconceivable to Paul that in the end the Jewish roots of God's saving plan, from which Paul himself emerged, would be tossed away. God had used the Jews to introduce salvation to the world. At the end-time Jews would find their place in God's heart.

THE FAILURE OF
THE ECUMENICAL DIALOGUE

Christianity had gone horribly awry, inflicting the horror of the Jewish journey from Christian-dominated cultures to the Holocaust. Hence Jews, in another strange and revolutionary way, became the arbiter of the Christian witness and salvation. Insofar as Christians persecuted Jews, Christianity ceased to be Christian. Since the persecution of Jews made up a significant part of Christian history, models of authentic Christianity were rare. Jews became those models for Christianity. It was Jewish values and steadfastness that could guide Christianity in the future.

In postwar Christianity, Jews embodied those who struggled, doubted, and affirmed God in the face of adversity and persecution. The Holocaust, supremely, highlighted this persecution and steadfastness. Jews who died were martyrs. Jews who survived became those who continued to affirm the newly created "Judeo-Christian tradition," in spite of everything. Jews as survivors could become the teachers of Christians on how to survive their own broken history. As it was in the beginning, Jews were the forerunners of Christianity. Now Jews and Christians would live salvation history together.

The appeal of Jews and Christians living together was mutual. The Holocaust had severely damaged the credibility of Christianity. Christians were in search of values and perspectives that would renew Christianity and make their faith credible again. The mass slaughters of Jews and the Christian desire to end the warfare of ideologies and religions made many Christians reevaluate the entire history of Christianity. The modern rise of secularism offered religious people escape from any and every religious community without penalty, and many Christians wondered why they should identify with a religion that answered less and less of the questions enlightened people were asking. Who wanted to carry the baggage of centuries of violence and atrocity?

Recognizing this situation, Christian theologians began analyzing Christian history and Christian theology to see if there was a way to remain Christian and retain credibility as a believer in the eyes of the Christian community and the wider world. Of course, some Christians believed that Christianity remained the one true religion, without change, and that history, even the history of the churches, had nothing to do with the eternal truths Christianity espoused. Other Christians thought that Christianity did represent and promulgate eternal truths but that those truths had to be thought through and translated to each new era in ways the world could recognize and affirm. Christians and the churches often strayed from the practices of compassion, forgiveness, and reconciliation that should flow from those truths. In the language of Vatican II, Christians should search for the signs of the times; these signs would guide Christians and the churches in the reconsideration and renewal of the Christian witness in the world.

Understandably, Jews were interested in the Christian witness insofar as it affirmed Jews. The initial aim of what became the Jewish-Christian dialogue was to get Christians off the backs of Jews and Judaism. Jewish leaders wanted the removal of any discrimination in society so that Jews could pursue their lives as equal and protected citizens. The American division of church and state prohibited the churches from direct influence in this area. However, since American society was overwhelmingly Christian, churches could provide an indirect, though significant, impetus for the integration of Jews into mainstream America. This would come primarily through how churches and church pastors viewed and talked about Jews.

The historical terrain of Christian witness had been so negative for Jews that we could not have foreseen the changes that occurred within decades after the Holocaust. There seemed to be little reason for Jews to reevaluate our theology and ritual. Judaism and Jews had held themselves together against great odds and had not transgressed against others. If Christianity needed reevaluation, Judaism did not. Christians might reintroduce Judaism and Jews into their theology and ritual, and they needed to listen and learn from Jews. However, we had little to learn from Christians and Christianity in the ecumenical dialogue. The ability of Christians to intrude forcefully into Jewish life was over. There would be no invitations to do so again.

Thus the ecumenical dialogue began. For Christians the dialogue mainly had to do with their religion and future. For Jews it mainly had to with supporting the Jewish community and its issues in society and the world. Jews asserted the right of Jews to define themselves apart from Christians both on the religious level and in the world. Anti-Semitism was the cornerstone issue, and Jews would monitor Christian movement in this area. Though Christians in large part agreed with the anti-Semitism litmus test, at first, the test criteria weren't clear. In the early days of the ecumenical dialogue, Israel was not central to Jewish identity. It only emerged as the central Jewish concern after the 1967 war.

Christian repentance for the Holocaust was the least controversial item on the agenda. The point was less a historical analysis of where culpability lay vis-à-vis the Nazis and more an overall judgment on Christian anti-Semitism. In America at least, the Nazis took second place with regard to the Holocaust. As a vanquished foe, the Nazis almost disappeared from view. Few people, except white supremacists, argued their innocence. Christians were the majority culture of Europe during the Nazi era. In the end, the separation of the Christian and Nazi parts of the Holocaust was shelved for an extended critique of historic Christian anti-Semitism. The Jewish beef with Christianity was longer and deeper.

By the 1970s, the framework of the ecumenical dialogue between Jews and Christians was established. Jewish leaders were less interested in settling historical scores than in the prospects for the future. Though the state of Israel had not yet been created when the Holocaust took place, and few Christian denominations had taken a stand on the Jewish community in Palestine before or during the Nazi years, Israel was now front and center in defining whether Christians had reformed their ways. In Holocaust theology and as put forth by Jewish leadership in the ecumenical dialogue, Israel was the place where support from Christians was necessary. Jews would define by ourselves who we were. Jews presented Israel as a religious issue, and Israel operated as the Jewish covenant in the contemporary world. The definition of contemporary anti-Semitism had been hammered out. This definition placed remembrance of the Holocaust and support for the state of Israel at the center of the Jewish agenda.

Christian theology and ritual had to be clarified. Because of anti-Semitism, Jews believed Christians had lost the right to define their internal life without the help of Jewish theologians and leadership. In some denominations there were rabbis and other Jewish leaders who held membership in a variety of Christian renewal committees. When it came time for Christians to rewrite policy statements and publish new religious education manuals, Jews were solicited for their expertise on such issues as how to interpret the Jewish scriptures and the Jewishness of Jesus. Jews advised Christians not only on presenting the universality of the Christian covenant without contravening Judaism, but also on discovering how Christianity could be enhanced by the continuation of the Jewish covenant.[3]

Israel was marked for special consideration. In the aftermath of the 1967 war, few Christians needed prompting from the Jewish community to celebrate that victory. With America bogged down in Vietnam and with the traditional Christian animosity toward Muslims and toward Third World peoples, the understanding was that Israel had won the 1967 war for all of us, Jews and Christians.

The war and Israel's lightning victory also reinforced the point that Israel was compensation for the Holocaust. The Christian world owed Jews Israel, and undivided economic and military support for this nascent Jewish state. Anti-Semitism still existed in the world, and Arabs were its primary carriers. Christians owed it to Jews to support Israel and to fight anyone who had picked up the virus of anti-Semitism that Christianity had created.

From the beginning, the ecumenical dialogue lacked a stable center that could sustain it over time. While Jews rightfully demanded full and independent recognition by their Christian counterparts, a lack of reciprocity was built into the dialogue itself. The lack of reciprocity had to do with the Jewish assertion of innocence in suffering *and* in empowerment, and with the static sense of Jewish identity that the Jewish delegates to the dialogue sought to instill in its deliberations. Decades after the Holocaust, Jews portrayed themselves as just emerging from the death camps. No elapsed time could change that feeling, nor could any change in Jewish or Christian life mitigate Christianity's inherent and always latent anti-Semitism. Any change would be corruption. It was as if the Jewish and Christian communities were frozen in time.

Jews assumed they were, and were presumed to be, representatives of Jewish history and especially the suffering within that history. That the Jews in the dialogue had been in America during the Holocaust or, as time went on, were born after the Holocaust, went without comment. Another obvious point was left out of the discussion: If Israel was so important to Jews, why had the Jewish delegates, who could become automatic citizens of the Jewish state upon their arrival in Israel, remained in the United States? If Israel could only be affirmed and any critique of Israel was forbidden, could the Christian delegates ask how the Jewish delegates could speak so freely and authoritatively about Israel without living there?

The Christians in the ecumenical dialogue were for the most part liberal in politics and on questions of racial and religious inclusion. They had opposed the Vietnam War and were critical of American militarism and imperialism. Their very participation in the dialogue was a sign of their liberality. The Jewish delegates were also liberal on the same issues. However, they were beginning to move in a more neoconservative political direction precisely because of their support for Israel and the policies and interests that they needed to speak for and attend to because of that support.

Christians spanned the globe, and because of this power, American Christians questioned Christian responsibility on the global scene. Balancing the parochial issues that the Jewish delegates raised with the broader issues facing the Christian delegates grew increasingly awkward over the years. Many of the Christian constituencies in the Third World, for example, were of necessity quite critical of American interventionism, capitalism, and support for repressive governments around the world. By the 1980s, and increasingly in the decades that followed, the Christian partners in the ecumenical dialogue broadened their horizons. The issues that Jews supported were much more parochial. Jewish horizons were narrowing.

The Jewish agenda was set: liberal on most any issue except Israel. Increasingly, the entire dialogue began to center around keeping criticism of Israel away from discussion. Thus Israel became the elephant in the dialogue room. To admit its presence was to risk ending the dialogue then and there. Though the Jewish delegates might be willing to do this, they would use this ending as evidence of renewed Christian anti-Semitism.

Christian participants in the ecumenical dialogue were afraid to speak lest they be responsible for harm coming to Jews. The Christian delegates wanted to avoid this at all costs and for a variety of reasons. Christians entered a tacit agreement with their Jewish partners and accepted the burden of self-censorship so that they could be redeemed by the Jews. First, most Christians in the ecumenical dialogue thought support for Israel was a Christian obligation after the Holocaust. Second, there was a fear of reisolating Jews. Jews and Christians should continue to relate to one another and remain in dialogue. Finally, most Christians knew little about the Middle East and, in the end, sided with the Jews they knew rather than the Palestinians and Arabs they didn't.

CHRISTIAN HOLOCAUST THEOLOGY

During the heyday of the ecumenical dialogue, Christians developed a viable and forceful complement to Jewish Holocaust theology. Led by theologians like Paul van Buren and Robert McAfee Brown, these thinkers sought to place Jews, the Holocaust, and Israel at the forefront of Christian consciousness. This Christian Holocaust theology brought together the strands of Christian renewal already mentioned. The Jewish scriptures were the Bible of Jesus; Jesus was a Jew and only a Jew; the history of Christianity against the Jews only made more visible the apostasy of Christianity to its own professed Lord and Savior; the Holocaust was the culmination of this Christian heresy; Israel was recompense for the suffering of the Jews and the litmus test to cleanse anti-Semitism from Christianity.

The centerpiece of Christian Holocaust theology was the need for Christian repentance toward the Jews. Since Christian repentance had often been offered in symbolic terms, this repentance could be achieved only through active support of Jewish causes in the present. At the height of this Christian Holocaust theology movement, Brown wrote a hagiographic biography of Elie Wiesel with the subtitle *Messenger to All Humanity*. Brown depicted Wiesel in terms used for a traditional Christian saint. Wiesel appeared as a re-

demptive figure, almost Christlike, who in his suffering offered redemption. Wiesel's suffering would be redemptive if
only the lessons that Wiesel taught were heeded. The Jewish
cause par excellence was Israel. Any movement away from
Israel by Christians was a forfeiture of redemption.[4]

The old Christian dichotomy between spirit and flesh or
faith and politics was once used against Jews in a negative
way. The idea that Christians were spiritual and holy, and
Jews were materialistic and carnal, reared its head again.
Holocaust theologians feared that some Christians who saw
religion as divorced from politics might mistake Israel as a
political cause, therefore shunning this commitment. This
was the very same mistake that Christianity had made in history. It was important for Christians to recognize the carnal
election of Israel. Repentant Christians could learn, in their
support of Israel, that the world is not divided into the spiritual and the material. The material world is the battleground
for spirituality. Israel is a material spirituality that Christians
need to support. In Christian Holocaust theology, support of
Israel is an obligation.

When looked in its entirety, Brown's work illustrates the
push and pull of the dialogue as it became a deal. Brown, a
great admirer of Wiesel, was also one of the early populariz-
ers of Latin American liberation theology for a North American Protestant audience. In book after book, Brown brought
the message of liberation with all its theological and political
ramifications to American Christians. Brown reached the
apex of popularity during the 1980s, when progressive Christians were protesting American interventionism in Central

America and organizing sanctuary movements for refugees fleeing to the United States. Brown spoke and wrote forcibly on this and other issues. Clearly, this brought Brown and others who shared his understanding into direct conflict with American foreign policy. Though Brown was always respectful, he was also consistent and forceful. As a Christian, he believed, justice had to be in the forefront. His responsibility as a Christian was to bring his faith to bear on his American citizenship.

Brown was an early supporter of the American-based Witness for Peace. This movement proposed placing American citizens in Nicaragua and elsewhere to oppose American interventionism against progressive governments that sought justice for the poor and marginalized. Soon the forces of Latin American liberation theology, which many Christians in America valued and listened to, drew the difficult but obvious conclusion that the Palestinians also needed liberation. Brown was caught in between, wanting justice for the oppressed, yet immensely troubled by almost two thousand years of anti-Semitism. Witness for Peace was suggested for the Israeli-occupied Palestinian territories. Since American foreign policy was heavily involved in supporting the Israeli occupation of an oppressed people, the issue was unavoidable. Could it be broached in the rarefied atmosphere of the Jewish-Christian dialogue deal?

Any Jew, myself included, who thought critically about Israel was seen as a dialogue breaker. As with other issues involving many communities, an ecumenical dialogue breaker was really an ecumenical deal breaker. Another equation had fallen; things weren't what they appeared to be. "The ecumenical dialogue equals the ecumenical dialogue" was false. What had begun in earnest in the 1950s and beyond, for good reason and with great expectations, had become a cover-up; "the ecumenical dialogue equals the ecumenical deal."

Perhaps it was inevitable. As Holocaust theology was once subversive, breaking through patterns of thought and challenging individual and communal assumptions, so too was the ecumenical dialogue. The idea, indeed the reality, that Jews and Christians could sit down at a table and speak frankly to one another about our mutual and difficult history and a joint future was amazing, indeed revolutionary. That this willingness to speak together came after such a cost seems to be part of the human drama. Still, there was a special poignancy as Jews and Christians finally broke bread together.

Christians deserve acclaim for their efforts, though only proportional to the disgrace of the previous years. Their motives were not entirely selfless. Without a new relationship with Jews, Christians lacked the internal strength or external credibility to continue as a credible faith. After the Holocaust, Christianity was at a crossroads. A history of violence was the road Christians knew well. Could Christianity become a religion of peace?

Judaism and Jewish leaders were moving in a different direction, perhaps inevitably. Jews needed to look out for themselves. After the Holocaust and after Israel, Jews could hardly afford a universal approach. The stakes were different; rather than credibility, for Jews the very survival of Jews and Judaism was at stake. The roads ahead for Jews and Christians, though in some ways converging, were also, in a fundamental way, divergent. Intent and honest in their desire to forge a new relationship, the partners in the ecumenical dialogue had different constituencies and needs. Even as Jews and Christians were talking with one another, they were also talking past one another.

A background unease with one another was left unspoken. As I traveled the country and the world, I met more than a few Christians who felt that the ecumenical dialogue had muzzled them. They resented the center of the dialogue become-deal that saw criticism of Israeli policy as a reason for accusations of anti-Semitism. Sometimes it was hard to figure out whether the silencing or the name-calling was more resented. For most, it came as a package deal and was received as such. Christian ecumenical dialogue participants felt keenly the need to silence the "anti-Semite."

Christians also resented becoming ecumenical *dealers*. Beneath and around the discussion I felt a new resentment toward Jews who "forced" Christians into silence. In book after book that came out announcing the triumph of the ecumenical dialogue, this unspoken resentment was absent. Over the years this resentment often morphed into other issues, like Jewish "control" of Congress, the power of the "Jewish" lobby, in short a feeling that Jews were powerful and were using that power to get "their" way.

Some Christians reverted to blaming *the* Jews. I asked the Christians who were complaining to me in private why they were silent. If Jews wanted them silenced to secure their own advantage, so be it. If in a supposed position of equality and dialogue Jews could "push" Christians around, then Christians deserved to be pushed. The point of the dialogue from the Jewish side was to speak up for what they wanted. Christians could do that as well. Wouldn't that help clarify the real issues at stake? Didn't every group have a right to pursue its own agenda? Especially in a dialogue setting, if power is being used unfairly or there is a perception that this is the case, doesn't the abused group have a responsibility to speak up for itself?

Over the years the ecumenical deal has made a shell of the original and revolutionary movement that generated the ecumenical dialogue. That Jews and Christians live together in relative harmony and security makes the dialogue possible. It also makes the deal possible. Since nothing personal or communal on the ground is at stake, at least in the actual lives of the participants, ecumenical dealers can hide as if the dialogue continues. They can attend meetings when they are called and just appear. Since Palestinians are thousands of miles away, they can be shut out of the picture. Should those who want good relations with their Jewish neighbors throw it all away for people who live half a world away? Aging and retired ecumenical dealers can also just drop off the scene. Institutional investments keep up the appearances of dialogue.

The last vestige of the ecumenical dialogue is Holocaust remembrance. On the local level, this often takes place in a Jewish house of worship, and sometimes Christians, in their churches, commemorate the Holocaust as well. Coupled with the older and varying councils of Christians and Jews, this annual event remains the mainstay of local ecumenical relations. On the national level, the Holocaust Memorial Museum in Washington, D.C., fulfills that function for institutionally affiliated members of the ecumenical dialogue.

At these gatherings, I see the fervor of joint declarations and commitments becoming routine, with less and less substance. The emotional years of reconciliation have passed, partly because time moves on and partly because the world of Jews and Christians has changed. The perpetually repeated reason for the commemoration of the Holocaust—that *never again* should anyone be silent in the face of injustice—mocks an ecumenical deal that calls for just that silence when it comes to injustices Jews are perpetrating against Palestinians. The only issue that is important to the Jewish ecumenical dialogists, Israel, is the only issue that can't be discussed honestly.

The excluded, the Palestinians, are the ecumenical deal breakers. Inviting a Palestinian to the dialogue or even speaking in the name of Palestinians is the ultimate deal-breaking heresy. But without even being there, Palestinians and Palestine have dominated the last years of the ecumenical dialogue. Jews and Christians can agree, as they often do, to table that issue out of respect for our common life together. If Jews table our dark side while demanding a continual return to the dark side of Christianity, can we expect respect, and can Jews respect Christians for cowering before us?

A reversal has taken place. In the Jewish-Christian dialogue, Christians have had much to repent for. They are, at the same time, plunging into the future. After having heard and internalized the moral challenges of the past, which they, for the most part, missed by a wide mark, what are their responsibilities now? If history is a judgment on Christianity, can Christians forge a future where that judgment upon them will change and they can afford to be silent again?

Historically, Christians have quite correctly been labeled oppressors. Many Christian theologians today are from groups historically oppressed by the church—women, the colonized, and the enslaved. These new theologians have challenged the oppressive history and ideas of Christianity, offered liberation theologies and ethics, and struggled, sometimes against conservative Christians, for a liberating Christianity. The Christian ecumenical participants are being asked to live up to the new confessions and pronouncements that changed their historical course. Changing course means changing decisions and loyalties. Christians now must decide which side they are on. Christian liberation theologies now challenge Christian Holocaust theology. Christian liberation theologies respond to historical contexts and the political conditions of the oppressed. Hence, liberation theologies are change-oriented and demand ever-new perceptions within changing contexts.

Holocaust theology is also contextual, and Christianity had to change to meet the needs that it now knows exist. History can't be changed. However, the present continues to change. Christians, adhering to their commitments, are changing as well. Jews are no longer helpless, and Israel, with the help of the Jewish establishment and the ecumenical dia-

logue, is now pursuing policies reminiscent of those condemned by all participants in the ecumenical dialogue. The
ecumenical deal is a secret known all over the block. Jews
seek to place a brake on the Christian perception of the
change in the Jewish condition by charging with anti-
Semitism anyone who articulates that change and the new
commitments demanded by the moment. Most Christians,
unfortunately, continue to accept that brake.

DIVESTING APARTHEID

The Reverend Fouad Abu-Akel is a Palestinian Christian
from inside Israel, meaning that his family is among one of
the remnant Palestinians who were not expelled in 1948.
Though these Palestinians remain within Israel and are Israeli citizens, they are second-class citizens at best. Few opportunities are provided to them; the restrictions they face
force many of the young to leave. As a young man, Abu-Akel
left Israel for America and later became a Presbyterian minister and an American citizen. In 2003, Abu-Akel was moder-
ator of the Presbyterian denomination when I was invited to
address the leaders of the Presbyterian leadership on my understanding of the ecumenical dialogue.

I first met Abu-Akel in 1990 when I co-hosted a tour of
Atlanta Christians to the Holy Land. Most such tourists are
interested in the holy sites, but new, justice-oriented tourists
also make time to meet what are called the "living stones" of
the land, Christian Palestinians. During our visit to the West
Bank, I met and began working with a number of Palestinian

Christians in their new venture, Sabeel, the Palestinian liberation theology center in Jerusalem. Over the years I worked and traveled with them.

Right before the Holy Land tour embarked, Naim Ateek and I delivered a series of lectures at a local Presbyterian church in Atlanta. I had met Ateek, a Palestinian Anglican priest, in Jerusalem in 1987 at the Shalom Hartman Institute, where I previewed my *Toward a Jewish Theology of Liberation* and was interrogated by Jewish interlocutors who had embraced the worst features of the ecumenical deal. Ateek's family, like that of Abu-Akel, remained in what became Israel. Thus, he is a Palestinian, an Israeli citizen, and a Christian clergyman. When I met him, Ateek was also the canon of St. George's Cathedral in Jerusalem.

After one lecture Ateek invited me to his home, where he presented me with a copy of his dissertation and asked if I would read and comment on it. The dissertation was a treatise on Palestinian liberation theology. The title was provocative—*Justice and Only Justice: A Palestinian Theology of Liberation*. I read the dissertation that night and agreed to take it back to Orbis Books at Maryknoll with the hope that they would publish it as a book.[5]

Ateek's book presented a Christian theology that left little if anything for a living Judaism. It was the opposite of what had become expected and accepted by Christians and Jews in the West. Ateek believed that with the coming of Jesus the Messiah, all the promises to the Jews, including the promise of the Land, had been abrogated. Jesus as the Christ superseded the old covenant; justice rather than the Land was now at the forefront. In the case of Israel, Jews were the aggressors and Palestinians the victims. God would make right the cause of the persecuted, and Jews, at some point, would be defeated. Still, Ateek argued for a compromise in his political program, a two-state solution, a courageous position for a Palestinian public figure at that time. I thought that his theology was regressive. Clearly, Ateek's theology had yet to be vetted and transformed by the exacting standards of the ecumenical dialogue. Yet it remained, at least historically, the mainstream Christian theological view of Jesus, the Jews, and the Land.

Ateek was the ecumenical dialogue's worst nightmare. Here was a Christian Palestinian whose theological premises had led to some of the most highly charged images of Jews in Christian history. He also had experienced Jews as vengeful conquerors in the flesh. Ateek challenged a mythic sense of powerless Jews with the real-time experience of Jews in power. In Atlanta, Ateek and I lectured on three consecutive evenings. Hundreds of people came each night to the church to hear us. The first Palestinian uprising was in full swing. Though the casualties were many, hope was in the air.

The audience was primarily white, while the delegation to Israel and Palestine was mixed. Almost half of our tour group was African American. The delegates included Lawrence Carter, the dean of the Martin Luther King Jr. International Chapel at Morehouse College. Like many prominent African Americans, Martin Luther King Jr. had attended Morehouse. Morehouse was and is on the cutting edge of Black history. It was and is heavily indebted to Jews for its founding, endowments, and faculty.

Our tour went to Israel/Palestine during the uprising. Palestinians stood up for their rights and paid the price for their resistance. The response of the tour's African Americans to these invigorating and sobering events matched that of a prominent civil rights leader who, some years earlier, had visited the area and referred to Palestinians as the "niggers" of the Middle East. He was duly chastised by Jewish leadership. Yet, the far less known African Americans on our tour understood the situation in the same way.

The ecumenical dialogue and deal had virtually no African American participants. Perhaps their identification with Palestinians was the reason. They also lacked the power to move in the higher circles of public life in America. The power elite is white Christian and Jewish. The comparison between Palestinian and African American life, so easy to make, is explosive. This is no doubt the reason for the policing of the South African Nobel laureate Desmond Tutu. As an activist within and a survivor of apartheid South Africa, Tutu had taken up the Palestinian cause many years earlier.

In 2007, Tutu became embroiled in an incident at the University of St. Thomas in Minneapolis. The university president revoked Tutu's invitation to speak on the "advice" of some members of the local Jewish community who accused Tutu of being anti-Israel and anti-Semitic. In the meantime, Professor Chris Toffolo, who had invited Tutu to speak and alerted him to the controversy that was brewing over his upcoming visit, was stripped of his position as chair of the university's Justice and Peace Program.

For years, Tutu had spoken out for Palestinians and against the Israeli occupation, seeing it as many others later did, as a policy akin to the apartheid he had struggled against. A few weeks after the brouhaha, Tutu wrote about his position on Israel:

> In our struggle against apartheid, the great supporters were Jewish people. They almost instinctively had to be on the side of the disenfranchised, of the voiceless ones, fighting injustice, oppression and evil. I have continued to feel strongly with the Jews. I am patron of a Holocaust centre in South Africa. I believe Israel has a right to secure borders.
>
> What is not so understandable, not justified, is what it did to another people to guarantee its existence. I've been very deeply distressed in my visit to the Holy Land; it reminded me so much of what happened to us black people in South Africa. I have seen the humiliation of the Palestinians at checkpoints and roadblocks, suffering like us when young white police officers prevented us from moving about.
>
> On one of my visits to the Holy Land I drove to a church with the Anglican bishop in Jerusalem. I could hear tears in his voice as he pointed to Jewish settlements. I thought of the desire of Israelis for security. But what of the Palestinians who have lost their land and homes?

I have experienced Palestinians pointing to what were their homes, now occupied by Jewish Israelis. I was walking with Canon Naim Ateek (the head of the Sabeel Ecumenical Centre) in Jerusalem. He pointed and said: "Our home was over there. We were driven out of our home; it is now occupied by Israeli Jews."

My heart aches. I say why are our memories so short? Have our Jewish sisters and brothers forgotten their humiliation? Have they forgotten the collective punishment, the home demolitions, in their own history so soon? Have they turned their backs on their profound and noble religious traditions? Have they forgotten that God cares deeply about the downtrodden?

Israel will never get true security and safety through oppressing another people. A true peace can ultimately be built only on justice. We condemn the violence of suicide bombers, and we condemn the corruption of young minds taught hatred; but we also condemn the violence of military incursions in the occupied lands, and the inhumanity that won't let ambulances reach the injured.

The military action of recent days, I predict with certainty, will not provide the security and peace Israelis want; it will only intensify the hatred.

Israel has three options: revert to the previous stalemated situation; exterminate all Palestinians; or—I hope—to strive for peace based on justice, based on withdrawal from all the occupied territories, and the establishment of a viable Palestinian state on those territories side by side with Israel, both with secure borders.

We in South Africa had a relatively peaceful transition. If our madness could end as it did, it must be possible to do the same everywhere else in the world. If peace could come to South Africa, surely it can come to the Holy Land?

My brother Naim Ateek has said what we used to say: "I am not pro- this people or that. I am pro-justice, pro-freedom. I am anti-injustice, anti-oppression."

But you know as well as I do that, somehow, the Israeli government is placed on a pedestal [in the United States], and to criticise it is to be immediately dubbed anti-Semitic, as if the Palestinians were not Semitic. I am not even anti-white, despite the madness of that group. And how did it come about that Israel was collaborating with the apartheid government on security measures?

People are scared in this country [the United States], to say wrong is wrong because the Jewish lobby is powerful—very powerful. Well, so what? For goodness' sake, this is God's world! We live in a moral universe. The apartheid government was very powerful, but today it no longer exists. Hitler, Mussolini, Stalin, Pinochet, Milosevic, and Idi Amin were all powerful, but in the end they bit the dust.

Injustice and oppression will never prevail. Those who are powerful have to remember the litmus test that God gives to the powerful: what is your treatment of the poor, the hungry, the voiceless? And on the basis of that, God passes judgment.

We should put out a clarion call to the government of the people of Israel, to the Palestinian people and say: peace is possible, peace based on justice is possible. We will do all we can to assist you to achieve this peace, because it is God's dream, and you will be able to live amicably together as sisters and brothers.[6]

I had the chance to stay the night in Abu-Akel's village, Kuffer-Yossif, twenty-five miles north of Nazareth. Though Kuffer-Yossif still has a Palestinian Israeli population and escaped the fate of the destroyed villages, Israel refuses to recognize most such surviving Palestinian villages. In practical terms this means that little or nothing is done to develop these villages, and municipal services to nonofficial villages are scant, a policy clearly intended to force Palestinians to leave so that the land can be taken by Jewish Israelis.

Something much more explosive was on the horizon, however. Behind the scenes, Presbyterians were working on a resolution for their 2004 General Assembly. The resolution proposed the following: an end to the Israeli occupation of Palestinian lands; mutual security guarantees; a negotiated equitable peace; an end to attacks on innocent people by both sides; the United States to be an evenhanded broker for peace; a United Nations peacekeeping force in Palestine; solidarity with their Christian partners in Israel/Palestine. Though much of this language had become the norm in various church bodies in the 1990s, this resolution, which passed by a wide margin, contained an even more explosive kicker at the end:

> 7. Refers to Mission Responsibility Through Investment Committee (MRTI) with instructions to initiate a process of selective divestment in multinational companies operating in Israel, in accordance to General Assembly policy on social investing, and to make appropriate recommendations to the General Assembly Council for action.[7]

With this resolution, Israel joined the Presbyterians' list of military-related and human rights investment policies they monitored. From that moment on, multinational companies doing business in the West Bank relating to the occupation of Palestinian land and human rights abuses would be recommended for disinvestment. The amount of money invested was less important than the pressure and publicity that could be applied on these issues. Noting the history of the Presbyterian Church applying its own values in these areas, the resolution was a shot across the bow of the ecumenical deal and the Jewish establishment. Israel was removed from the hands-off list and could no longer count on the evenhanded, "balanced" approach that criticized both sides without speaking boldly about Israeli's abuse of Palestinian human rights.

After these long years, finally, some Christians had broken the ecumenical deal—in public, before the world. Though the action was largely symbolic, I knew that the Jewish establishment and Christians whose bread and butter was the ecumenical deal would instantly note the power of the symbolism. Sure enough, a barrage of catcalls as predictable as they were loud greeted the resolution. The main criticisms revived the old charge of Christian anti-Semitism.

National and local Jewish institutions activated a full-court press against the resolution. They sent local rabbis to local Presbyterian churches, using the same lines of communications that supported interfaith councils and Holocaust remembrance events. Jewish officials as well as ordinary congregants communicated their sense of betrayal to church members, who, for the most part, were unaware of the controversy and were certainly against anything that would harm local interfaith relationships. The national leadership of the Presbyterian Church was also inundated with publicity that raised the question of "singling" out Israel and anti-Semitism.

By their next General Assembly in 2006, the Presbyterians were on the defensive. While they held some of their ground, refusing a recommendation to repeal and rescind the actions of the previous assembly related to the "phased selective divestment in multinational corporations operating in Israel," they adopted different language. The assembly reset the church's policy, directing that "financial investments of the Presbyterian Church (U.S.A.), as they pertain to Israel, Gaza, East Jerusalem, and the West Bank, be invested in only peaceful pursuits." The shift was one of tone. They changed divestment—with its obvious comparison with apartheid South Africa, whose central focus was overturning an unjust system—to investments for peace; the language was much less confrontational and more suggestive.

On the eve of the 2008 General Assembly, members of the Jewish establishment sent a letter to the Presbyterians. Its central ideas were drawn from Holocaust theology. Though tempered by the changing international debate raging about Israeli policies toward the Palestinians, it remained wedded to the myths of Israel that Flapan and other Israeli historians had debunked decades ago. The letter began with the mutual desire of the Jewish and Christian communities to lessen human suffering and acknowledged how both communities shared the same goals of peace and harmony. On divestment, the heart of the resolution, the gloves came off.

> 3. Such a process ends up being linked with the anti-Apartheid activities that once united us. In fact, the mantra of many of Israel's detractors has been to draw repeated parallels, including terminology ("apartheid fence") and strategy ("sanctions and divestment"). The purpose of the anti-Apartheid divestment strategy was to delegitimize and end the Apartheid regime. It will be impossible to disabuse most Jews, here and in Israel, and the American public that no such comparison is meant.
>
> 4. Divestment may well undermine willingness by Israelis to imagine peace. While we recognize that Israel is a nation with a powerful military, it is

important to remember that terror is a weapon of great and devastating power—with lasting consequence. Decades of terror and international isolation since 1948 have left Israelis feeling threatened and isolated. Divestment, with all of its historical connotations, seriously threatens to deepen that isolation. Together and independently, Christians, Jews, and Muslims must give the parties to the conflict the confidence they need to move toward peace. For the Israelis, concessions on land, settlements, the relaxation of security and the resulting improved conditions for Palestinians will not come as the result of further isolation. History has shown that the greatest strides by the Israelis have come as the result of international support. Divestment as a policy is more likely to provoke and less likely to build trust and understanding.

5. Divestment validates and supports Palestinian intransigence by giving hope that, ultimately, the world will allow Israel to be destroyed and Palestinian extremist dreams realized. Most Israelis feel, and we agree, that much terrorism is grounded in a rejection of Israel's right to exist—one reason why attacks increased during the period following the signing of the Oslo Accords. Palestinian terrorism, before 1967 and since, has targeted schools, buses, cafes, discothèques, hotels—places where innocents, particularly children and families, congregate. We fear that terrorism may continue after the cre-

ation of a Palestinian state, especially if it appears
that independence for the Palestinians came as the
result of terrorism rather than negotiations. Peace
will not come until, along with the return of territory,
there is a commitment on the part of the Palestinians
to destroy the terrorist infrastructure, recognize Israel's right to exist, foreswear violence, and commit
to expressing grievances without the use of terror
and other forms of violence. The primary responsibility for ending extremist terrorism rests with the
Palestinian leadership. Any policy that gives Palestinian extremists hope that they can wait until Israel
is weakened prolongs the agony and will exacerbate
violence.[8]

Here was what was left of Holocaust theology. Battered
and no longer plausible in its entirety—notice that there is no
claim that Israel is completely innocent—there remains only
the sense that, even with Israel's power, it is a victim of aggression. Israel is attacked for no reason except Palestinian
"intransigence" that feeds extremism and terrorism. The
"decades of terror and international isolation since 1948"
make Israel feel vulnerable despite its power. How then can
Israelis "imagine peace"?

Presbyterians, in comparing Israel to apartheid South
Africa, encourage the Palestinians to believe, like South
African Blacks, that their cause can be won, that they can
delegitimize Israel's oppression and, with allies like the Presbyterians, eliminate the Jewish state. The Presbyterians were

duly warned: by acting to divest from corporations that participate in the occupation of West Bank Palestinian land, Christians might be signing the death warrant of the Jewish state and with it millions of Jews. This warning went against a plain reading of the resolution—and all previous ones of the General Assembly—affirming Israel's right to exist in freedom and security.

After September 11, Islam was added to the ecumenical dialogue, but an Islam stripped of its primary concerns outside of assimilation to America and the Judeo-Christian ethos. Muslims were added to combat encroaching secularism and religious fundamentalism in America. The dialogue was mostly about learning how Muslims prayed; how they interpreted the Koran; their relationship, if there was any, to the Jewish and Christian scriptures; and how the three monotheistic religions could provide a joint stand against religious intolerance and terrorism. These terms determined Islam's inclusion in the ecumenical dialogue.

In the aftermath of September 11, the ecumenical deal was further solidified, even as it was breaking apart. On the one hand, Christians and Jews who saw their future tied together against the threat of Islamic terrorism saw Israel as an early warning of what had now come home to the United States. The liberalizing agenda of listening to voices outside of the West had opened doors to the barbarians at the gates. Was there anyone left to guard them? On the other hand, other Christians, having listened to voices from around the world, thought that still more listening was needed. What exactly were the grievances of people, including some Mus-

lims, who experienced the underside of the global economic
order? Rather than simply condemning terrorism, shouldn't
we listen to those voices and see what, if any, truths were
there to consider?

Jews of Conscience joined these latter voices. They had
been frozen out of the ecumenical dialogue from the start,
and as the ecumenical deal took hold, both sides of the dialogue condemned Jewish and Christian dissenters as part of
the ecumenical deal. In some ways, condemnation of deal
breakers was the only life left in the dialogue itself. Joint
condemnation gave religious and political coverage to the
ecumenical partners while spreading culpability among the
participants. Though such condemnation made some participants nervous, it further invested each party in continuing,
at least on paper, a joint effort to defend Judeo-Christian
values. In defense of those values, the idea of a "clash of civi-
lizations" became almost a mantra. Fundamentalist Islam
had already entered Europe and was at the doorstep of
America. Being on the Judeo-Christian side of the clash
became a calling card for status and, indeed, sanity among
dialogue participants.

Over the years the Muslim population had increased in
the United States, and it was now approaching the size of the
Jewish population. After September 11, American universities began adding or increasing Islamic studies programs. All
vested parties, including Muslims anxious to assimilate to the
West, proposed a division between militant Islam and mainstream Islam. In recognition of the increasing number of
Muslims in the United States as well as of the increasing im-

portance of Islam worldwide, some Jews and Christians initiated mainstream Muslims into the ecumenical dialogue.
There was genuine interest in reaching out to Muslims.
However, suspicions remained about whether the stated
aims of mainstream Muslims were their real aims. The pars-
ing of Islam continues with a separation of two branches:
backward and fundamentalist Islam versus moderate, peace-
loving Islam. Those Muslims called to the ecumenical table
are the moderates, who, like their Christian counterparts,
are called to condemn their shadow side.

The ecumenical dialogue partners understand that such
dialogue is an integrating factor in achieving a normal and ordinary life together. The mythology of America is that it is
different from other societies in the ability of diverse people
to live side by side with difference. The increasing number of
Muslims challenges that myth, which depends partly on how
Muslims fit or don't fit into the Judeo-Christian civilization.
Who decides this fitness?

Jews decide. Do Jews decide? And if Jews decide, which
Jews? Jews are the gatekeepers of the ecumenical dialogue/
deal; Christians are their junior partner. Jews historically
have had an ambivalent, though on the whole positive, relationship with Islam and Muslim power. Christians and
Muslims have often butted up against one another for geographic, religious, and political space. True, Jews have been
second-class citizens under Islamic rule, yet they have
avoided the wholesale persecution they often experienced
under Christian domination. Whatever the intent and cir-
cumstance, nothing approaching the Holocaust ever oc-

curred under Islamic rule. Muslims were not among the rulers of the death camps. Auschwitz was a Christian, European, German, Nazi event. Only Christian holy days, including Christmas, were celebrated at Auschwitz.

Israel, a primary concern for Muslims, and from their perspective the dark side of Judaism, still remains off the table. While Islamic terrorism can be discussed endlessly, Israeli terrorism can never be broached. The reason for this lack of discussion of Israeli terrorism is Jewish power and the assertion that Israel stands as a bulwark against terrorism. A deeper reason remains implicit: Who, except the uncivilized, could even suggest a connection between Israel and terrorism? The two are antithetical. Who but the savage anti-Semites of the world could even pose such a canard? And who, Christian or Jew, could listen to such mindless and dangerous rhetoric except anti-Semites parading as upstanding Christians and Jews?

4

Mapping Jewish Destiny

News in the Middle East seems endlessly recycled. Who among us remembers the Wye River Memorandum of October 1998? It was just one among many other agreements to "solve" the Israeli-Palestinian crisis. The Wye Memorandum carried forth the January 1997 Hebron Protocol. Hebron was a corollary to the Interim Agreement of September 1995, itself a corollary to the Oslo Accords of 1993. Oslo came in response to the Madrid Conference of 1991.

It seems that the "peace process" is endless. But to what end? Another round in the peace process took place in Annapolis, Maryland, in November 2007. As usual, the Israeli side made beautiful speeches and the Palestinian side lamented its people's suffering. When over, the daylong meeting joined a long list of other "significant" peace efforts. All these decades of agreements and agreements-not-to-agree led to the present impasse. In a few years, who will remember Annapolis?

I remember Wye because I wrote an editorial on its failure, as it was being signed. The memorandum failed, as did my editorial, which sought to galvanize public opinion for policies that might herald an ordinary life for both Jews and Palestinians. I wrote for another reason as well. I wanted to move discussion beyond the predictable rhetoric that had characterized all sides of the conflict. I thought maps should be the reference point for any further discussion of a way forward.[1]

Maps are crucial. If we look at maps as reports on our personal and collective condition, we can visualize where we are. Looking at previous maps in relation to present ones, we can appreciate where we have come from. Then we can map where we want to be in the future. Mapping tells us more than rhetorical flourishes. Or if rhetorical flourishes are necessary for our psyche, even for the saving of face, maps are sobering. Though some factors cannot be mapped in a conventional material way, maps are indispensable aids, especially when history and emotion make seeing a more objective reality difficult or impossible.

If all parties looked at the maps of Israel, we would gain concrete pictures of where people, land, institutions, settlements, roads, and territories appeared or disappeared. We could see what life means for Israelis and Palestinians. In mapping, each side would, of course, tend to highlight the maps that benefit it and bury the maps that challenge it. Looking at more and more maps with sober maturity, however, we would also see those that indict our self-righteousness. If we judge them by the standard of the kind of life anyone would want for himself and for others, they would tell us that things need to be rearranged. Then we could develop a mechanism to achieve that goal.

Three Jewish maps stand out in the contemporary world and depict who Jews have become in recent history. They show the formative events of the Holocaust, the ethnic cleansing of Palestinians in the creation of Israel, and the permanent Israeli occupation being maintained and extended in the West Bank. What shall we do in light of these maps? They are intimately related to the Israeli-Palestinian conflict, yet, like most significant mappings of a people, they move far beyond the immediate problem at hand.

The map of the Holocaust is enshrined in Jewish life, and many around the world know it. This map of Europe today has only a remnant of surviving Jewish communities found there after the systematic murder of six million Jews and the destruction of the indigenous life of European Jewry. This concrete picture of the Holocaust is not a map only for Jews. The map of Jewish death is also the map of Germans and Europeans. After all, they created the map of the Holocaust; it represents their will and the powers that murdered millions of Jews.

Palestinians and their supporters around the world know the second map. Over four hundred Palestinian villages were destroyed in the ethnic cleansing of the Palestinians, and hundreds of thousands of Palestinians were driven from their land, never to return. In the 1990s, Salman Abu-Sitta, a Palestinian refugee, researched, drew, and published a detailed map of the lost villages of Palestine. His work reminds Palestinians of where they once lived. This map is also a map for Israelis and Jews everywhere, since Jews inflicted that cleansing and defended it.[2]

The third map shows the permanent extension of Israel into the West Bank, depicting all of its accompanying support structures. It is a picture of what Jewish settlers have built and of where they live on other people's land through their displacement of Palestinians and the resulting loss of Palestinian land, livelihoods, and hope. This map demarcates quite distinctly the barriers, fences, and walls that invade and surround Palestinians in Jerusalem and the West Bank. Israelis set these final demarcations in place *after* the Wye River Memorandum.

Maps made at the time of Wye show the challenge and the reality of what has become even worse since. Prime Minister Benjamin Netanyahu and Minister of Defense Ariel Sharon presented a map at Wye as their vision of the settlement of the conflict between Israel and the Palestinians. It drew the boundaries of Palestinian and Jewish life and their collective future—after all, the future of Israel/Palestine and the future of the Jewish and Palestinian people were and are intertwined. This map, this challenge of a joint future, is what now most Jewish religious, intellectual, and political leaders refuse to acknowledge. Within the continuing expansion of Israel, it marked the boundaries of Jewish life in Israel and the Diaspora at the dawn of a new century. The Annapolis Conference glossed over this Wye map.

The carving up of the West Bank into Israeli-controlled settlements and discrete Palestinian population centers is hardly new. The expansion of Israel and the diminution of land inhabited and controlled by Palestinians began with the founding of Israel in 1948 and the partition of Israel and realities. First, there were the security zones under Israel's control: twenty kilometers to the west of the Jordan River; ten kilometers from the pre-1967 borders of Israel to Palestinian-controlled land. These zones spread the length of Israel and the Palestinian areas. They were designed to insure military security from Palestinian attacks and prevent a consolidation of Palestinian areas with Jordan. Second, there were areas to be controlled by Palestinians. They were sandwiched between the Israeli security zones and were divided north and south through Israeli control of Jerusalem. The security zones and the divided Palestinian centers thus limited, in the most fundamental geographic and political ways, Palestinian autonomy. What passed for Palestinian autonomy resembled an apartheid Bantustan-like system rather than a state.

The Wye map is the same map presented to Palestinians ever since. The map shows, within the pre-1967 borders of Israel, a continual pattern of Israeli control and Palestinian life lived within the borders of a Jewish state and a continually shrinking remnant of the original Palestinian presence before the establishment of the state. Within Israel, a population that numbers over a million Arabs is defined as second-class citizens. Just as the Palestinians within Israel are part of a remnant population displaced and expelled in the formation of Israel, so too is the Palestinian population of the West Bank, numbering about two and a half million persons. The Netanyahu-Sharon map charts the areas where these two remnant populations will live for the foreseeable future.

This map represents a permanent occupation of the West Bank and, as a proposed final settlement with the

Palestine. It continued with the annexation of Jerusalem an
the occupation of the West Bank and Gaza after the 1967 wa
The Allon Plan, formulated just months after the 1967 wa
already envisioned a further permanent expansion of Israe
into the West Bank. Israel was to appropriate as much of th
West Bank water and land as possible with, for demograph
reasons, the least number of Palestinians. The maintenanc
of a Jewish majority in Israeli-controlled land would lea
Palestinian population centers encircled by new and e
panding Jewish settlements. In other words, in the Allon Pl
and those that followed, Palestinian population centers we
limited to reservation-type enclaves. Thus the Netanyah
Sharon map should be seen in historical perspective as a co
tinuation of 1948 and 1967, differing from Prime Minist
Yitzhak Rabin's and Simone Peres's Oslo map only in mir
details.[3]

The Wye Memorandum represented a consensus of
raeli leadership and public opinion. Because the Wye Me
orandum was most often analyzed as a product of Netany
and Sharon, rather than in its historical continuity, its sigr
cance was lost on the general public and the Jewish com
nity as well. Contrary to Jewish liberal opinion, Netany
essentially adopted an Oslo peace process that was initi
by the prior Labor government at Wye, as did Sharon,
became prime minister in 2001. Though progressive
saw Sharon as outside the consensus of Israeli politic
was, until his debilitating stroke in 2006, involved in pol
leadership in every administration during his adult life.

The Wye Memorandum consolidated two fundam

Palestinian leadership, legalizes the occupation as inside the new borders of Israel. The Wye Memorandum envisioned the end of the Israeli occupation of the West Bank through the expansion of Israel's boundaries to the Jordan River. The autonomous Palestinian areas within and outside the pre-1967 borders of Israel were redefined as within the expanded Israeli state. The occupation ended when it was made part of state policy, thus legalizing what has been declared illegal by international law.

Palestinians in Jerusalem, the West Bank, and Gaza (though Gaza was a special case then and still is now), previously autonomous, were circumscribed within an expanded Israel, and added to the Palestinian population within the pre-1967 borders of Israel. Unlike the earlier group, however, these Palestinians were without even second-class citizenship. Besides a technical detail or two, the post-Wye maps differ little. They indeed are in a continuum with the maps presented by Yitzhak Rabin or those who have come after Netanyahu: Ehud Barak, Ariel Sharon, Ehud Olmert, and beyond.

THE BOUNDARIES OF JEWISH DESTINY

The many post-Wye maps show increasingly *less* land and opportunity for Palestinians, and the Separation Wall now demarcates and enforces the boundaries. Without a plan that reverses Wye and everything that came before and has come since, no matter what the rhetoric on either side, the situation will become permanent. Israel will stretch from Tel Aviv to the Jordan River, with two remnant populations of Palestinians within its borders, and the Gaza Strip will remain either imprisoned as a third remnant or become one of the two categories of Palestinians within Israel. Jews of Conscience stand within the ruins of Constantinian Judaism. They study these maps, mourn for the loss of Jewish ethics, and wonder what is next for the Palestinians, for them, and for Jewish life.

The future of Judaism and Jewish life is traced on the current map of Israel. The boundaries for Palestinians and Israelis threaten to become the boundaries of Jewish life, and in a strange and ironic twist, they may become the boundaries of Jewish destiny. The reduction of Palestine to three remnant populations will make faithful Jews also a remnant, as these two remnants now travel together within Jewish life. Remnants are demographic categories, and indeed, the maps show the Palestinian population as a remnant. Remnant Jews must look at these maps and draw the obvious conclusion: Jewish life as we have known and inherited it and Jewish life as it is presented to Jews and others in the world is, for all practical purposes, over. Only Constantinian Judaism and Jews of Conscience remain.

Political maps show a bonding of flesh and blood lurking beneath the surface of power politics. The maps, with their political borders, are drawn from a common experience of power exercised and endured with great suffering. The intertwined destiny of Palestinian and Jew is still to be found in the recognition of the violation of others and in the confessions contained therein. First is the map of the Holocaust, then the map of Jewish empowerment, within which lie stories of suffering. Some of these stories involve what at first glance seem to be comparisons of the Holocaust and what Jews have been doing to Palestinians. As I uncovered these shocking stories, I found the myths I held as a Jew undermined, and they became stories of the confession I was drawn to make.

These "comparison" stories, on a deeper reading, express something other than a comparison; they reference a taboo and confront it out loud: Jews are continuing the very cycle of violence and atrocity perpetrated against us. What has our history come to? The stories challenge us, in our empowerment, with a stark choice. We can use our power to end the cycle of violence and atrocity as our leaders and theologians once hoped, or we can continue to use our power to repeat that cycle under cover of our banners and ideologies.

After I finished *Toward a Jewish Theology of Liberation*, and with the Palestinians uprising in full swing, stories of Israelis' abuse of Palestinian human rights filled the pages of magazines and newspapers in Israel and America. I read these stories with horror and amazement. Three stories stand out as challenges to end the cycle of violence and atrocity. The first is from the 1948 war and the others are from the first Palestinian uprising itself.

After the first Palestinian uprising began, Amos Kenan, a columnist for the Israeli daily *Yediot Aharonot*, wrote "Four Decades of Blood Vengeance," a dialogue with George Habash, head of the Popular Front for the Liberation of Palestine. Kenan met Habash in 1948, when the Israeli army conquered Lydda. A soldier at the time, Kenan was a part of the invading and occupying force that kept Palestinian Arabs at a distance. Habash, whose ailing sister lived in Lydda, managed to avoid Israel's security system to visit her. She was thirty years old, married, with six children, and deathly ill. A medical doctor, Habash prescribed the appropriate medicines, but because Lydda was under curfew, his sister had no access to pharmacies and died three days later. The curfew also prevented her proper burial. Habash dug a grave with his own hands and buried his sister in her own backyard. When Israel lifted the curfew, it transferred the survivors of the village, Habash and his sister's six children included, to temporary prison compounds from which they were later expelled to Jordan.

Kenan recalled his days of guard duty in Lydda as essentially uneventful. He found them at times comical because of the lack of military preparedness of those soldiers who had recently arrived from Eastern Europe and who had weapons of dubious quality. Since most of the inhabitants of Lydda had fled before the Jewish soldiers' occupation, few military personnel were left to guard the Arab villagers who remained. The bored soldiers did much standing around and gossiping. But they did more horrifying things as well:

> In the afternoon, those of us who couldn't take it any more would steal off to Tel Aviv for a few hours, on one excuse or another. At night, those of us who couldn't restrain ourselves would go into the prison compounds to fuck Arab women. I want very much to assume, and perhaps even can, that those who

couldn't restrain themselves did what they thought the Arabs would have done to them had they won the war.

Once, only once, did an Arab woman—perhaps a distant relative of George Habash—dare to complain. A court martial trial was called. The accused, who was sitting behind the judges, signaled to the woman by running the back of his hand across his throat. She understood and did not testify. The rapist was not acquitted; he simply was not accused, because no one would accuse him. Two years later, someone killed him while he plowed the fields of an Arab village, one no longer on the map because its inhabitants fled and left it empty.

Kenan wrote about blood vengeance and about how difficult it was to square accounts. Many sought and took revenge, and, to his mind, all the vengeance had already come:

Both you and I, George, have already taken vengeance—before and during and after the fact. And both you and I have not taken pity on man or woman, boy or girl, young or old. I know that there is not much difference between pressing a button in a fighter plane and firing point blank into the head of a hostage. As there is no difference between a great massacre that was not meant to be and one that was meant to be. There is no distinction between justice and justice or between injustice and injustice, as

there is no difference at all in what people—weak,
transient beings, assured of the justice of their ways
and their deeds—are capable of doing to people who
are in sum exactly like themselves.

Tears filled my eyes, George, when I read for the
first time in these forty years how your sister died.
How you dug her a pit with your own hands in the
yard of her house in the city of Lydda. I reach out
with an unclean hand to your hand, which also is not
clean. You and I should die a miserable natural
death, a death of sinners who have not come to their
punishment, a death from old age, disease, a death
weak and unheroic, a death meant for human beings
who have lived a life of iniquity.[4]

Two other stories from the Palestinian uprising make
clearer this connection between Palestinian and Jewish
Holocaust history. The first story, from January 1988, occurred a month after the Palestinian uprising had begun,
when an Israeli captain was summoned to his superior. The
captain was instructed to carry out arrests in the village of
Hawara, outside Nablus—such arrests of innocent young
Palestinians were hardly out of the ordinary. However, the
further instructions were disturbing. Out of conscience, the
officer refused the instructions, so they were turned into a direct order. Then the captain, with a company of forty soldiers, boarded a civilian bus at Hawara at eleven o'clock in
the evening.

The local *muhktar* or "chosen" head of a village, given a

list of twelve persons, rounded them up, and the twelve sat on the sidewalk in the center of the village, offering no resistance. Yossi Sarid, an Israeli politician and political analyst, describes what followed.

> The soldiers shackled the villagers, and with their hands bound behind their backs they were led to the bus. The bus started to move and after 200–300 meters it stopped beside an orchard. The "locals" were taken off the bus and led into the orchard in groups of three, one after another. Every group was accompanied by an officer. In the darkness of the orchard the soldiers also shackled the Hawara residents' legs and laid them on the ground. The officers urged the soldiers to "get it over with quickly, so that we can leave and forget about it." Then, flannel was stuffed into the Arabs' mouths to prevent them from screaming and the bus driver revved up the motor so that the noise would drown out the cries. Then the soldiers obediently carried out the orders they had been given: to break their arms and legs by clubbing the Arabs; to avoid clubbing them on their heads; to remove their bonds after breaking their arms and legs, and to leave them at the site; to leave one local with broken arms but without broken legs so he could make it back to the village on his own and get help.[5]

The beatings were so fierce that most of the wooden clubs were broken. Thus was born the title of the article about this action, "The Night of the Broken Clubs," an allusion to the Nazi Kristallnacht, the Night of Broken Glass.

The second story occurred just months after the beatings, when Marcus Levin, a physician, was called up for reserve duty in the Ansar prison camp. When he arrived, Levin met two colleagues and asked for information about his duties. The answer: "Mainly you examine prisoners before and after an investigation." Levin responded in amazement, "After the investigation?" which prompted the reply, "Nothing special, sometimes there are fractures. For instance, yesterday they brought a twelve-year-old boy with two broken legs." Dr. Levin then demanded a meeting with the compound commander and told him, "My name is Marcus Levin and not Josef Mengele, and for reasons of conscience I refuse to serve in this place." A doctor who was present at the meeting tried to calm Levin: "Marcus, first you feel like Mengele, but after a few days you get used to it." An article written about this incident was called "You Will Get Used to Being a Mengele."[6]

The references to Kristallnacht and to the Nazi physician Mengele to describe contemporary Jewish Israeli policy and activity startled me. They still do today. That the Jewish community resists this Nazi analogy is understandable; it hopes to silence all such references. Yet, from the very beginning of the Jewish struggle for statehood in Palestine in the 1940s until today, Jewish Israelis have repeatedly made the connection between the Jewish experience of suffering in Europe and the Palestinian experience of suffering at the hands of the Jewish people in Palestine and Israel. It remains with us. It is part of the Jewish future.

Over the years I have tried to understand the meaning of these Nazi references. Though difficult to fathom, they are not primarily comparisons between Nazi and Israeli behavior, though some of the Nazis' pre-1938 behavior may be comparable. They are not attempts to further political objectives, such as promoting one political party over another. They are not challenges to the legitimacy of the state of Israel.

The force of the Nazi reference is in the intuitive link between the historic suffering of the Jews and the present suffering of Palestinians. It conveys an implicit recognition of the injustices, once committed against Jews, that Jews are now committing against another people. This connection is prepolitical and preideological. It operates in a terrain filled with images of Jewish and Palestinian suffering. The political "realities" of the situation, the need to be "strong," or even the communal penalties for speaking the truth do not quiet this deeper intuitive connection.

It is impossible today to understand the totality of the Jewish discussion, filled with martyrs, exile, and the Holocaust, unless Jews include as their intimate partners those whom we too have tortured, expelled, and murdered. The Nazi reference is a plea to end a madness that was visited upon Jews for millennia, which now Jews visit upon another people.

Jews can be liberated from policies and attitudes that are betrayals of Jewish history. Such liberation would release

Jews from theologies that currently serve to close off critical thought and favor the powerful at the expense of others. In the truth of potential mutual destruction are the seeds of possibility and the hope of moving into an engaged struggle on behalf of the history of the Jewish and the Palestinian peoples. To seek to escape such destruction is not weakness, lack of political maturity, or even self-hate; it is a call to use power morally.

With whom can we end these cycles of violence and atrocity if not with our "enemy"? Is it possible to relinquish the enemy dividing lines, the designation of each side as Jews or Palestinians? The two polarized identities have become so dear to each side and to its partisans that they make it difficult to see what is best for both and to find a way forward. I have come to think that my own moral and ethical arguments from the Jewish tradition might retard the process of seeking peace with justice. Likewise, Palestinian identity, with its own history, can also be a distraction, and Palestinians need freedom to chart their own destiny without being caught up in the Muslim symbolism that others, whether Islamic or anticolonial countries, have imposed on them. That mythology holds their freedom in bondage to others who do not suffer the consequences of infinite delay and intractable intransigence.

Perhaps we can recognize that our enemy is somewhere else: within the boundaries and borders drawn for us by "our" leaders. The challenge before us is to end those cycles once and for all. Rearranging these borders is rearranging the boundaries of our future. We owe this rearranging to those who have suffered in the past and still suffer in the present.

CONFESSING IN THE PRESENCE OF
THE BURNING CHILDREN

The voices of those who could not take it anymore have increasingly grown silent. As the years pass, we hear fewer and fewer gripping narratives and disturbing analogies: the rape of Palestinian women, the outstretched unclean hand, the Night of the Broken Clubs. After a while we get used to it: "My name is Marcus Levin and not Josef Mengele." Even as the maps I described have made their way into newspapers as prestigious as the *New York Times*, our framework for understanding these stories and information is still lacking.

Frameworks for understanding conflict often distort reality, sometimes unintentionally, other times purposefully. Frameworks come into being when they help to articulate important personal and communal questions that previous understandings, overwhelmed by events, can no longer handle. At their best, frameworks pose the crucial questions we need to ask. When a history of suffering is involved, the urgency for a new framework of understanding becomes a consuming passion. With the suffering in the present and more in the offing, everything is on the line, and, consequently, everything is up for grabs.

When everything is up for grabs, the stakes are high. Life is the highest stake, but that stake raises the question of what makes life worth living. The search for answers is beset with complexity; gray areas abound when life and meaning are closely examined. Maps, too, contain gray areas that must be attended to, though certain boundaries are drawn. Though these boundaries contain more questions and are open for further exploration, the boundaries themselves represent different decisions in light of new information. Thus, boundaries are interpretative frameworks on the move.

In the 1980s, the stories of the founding of Israel and Israel's repression of the first Palestinian uprising compelled me to seek a new interpretative framework for the future of Israel/Palestine and Jewish life: what first struck me there has continued unabated. Jews have arrived at an increasingly neoconservative politics in America; the consolidation and expansion of Israel in Jerusalem and the West Bank has occurred; the search for various forms of anti-Semitism, including an ever-evolving discussion of the "new" anti-Semitism, has intensified.

There were and are other possibilities, roads not taken. The Holocaust bequeathed to us two fundamental lessons: Never again should anything like the Holocaust happen to the Jewish people, and never again should anything like the Holocaust happen to any people. As Irving Greenberg wrote in 1974: "The Holocaust asks above all else not to allow the creation of another matrix of values that might sustain another attempt at genocide." Greenberg also warned against using the Holocaust as a form of triumphalism:

Its moral challenge must also be applied to Jews. Those Jews who feel no guilt for the Holocaust are also tempted to moral apathy. Religious Jews who use the Holocaust to morally impugn every other religious group but their own are the ones who are tempted into indifference at the Holocaust of others (cf. the general policy of the American Orthodox rabbinate on United States Vietnam policy). Those Israelis who place as much distance as possible between the weak, passive Diaspora victims and the "mighty Sabras" are tempted to use Israeli strength indiscriminately beyond what is absolutely inescapable for self-defense and survival, which is to risk turning others into victims of the Jews. Neither faith nor morality can function without a serious twist of perspective, even to the point of becoming demonic, unless they are illumined by the fires of Auschwitz and Treblinka.[7]

Faith and morality must be illumined by the fires of Auschwitz and Treblinka—and Vietnam, Cambodia, Rwanda, Sudan, Iraq, and Palestine. This option has been buried for too long.

Greenberg's other faith assertion has been quoted for years: "After Auschwitz, no statement, theological or otherwise, should be made that would not be credible in the presence of the burning children." To use Jewish history as a form of triumphalism and oppression is exactly the opposite of his faith proposal. We can have only the political, economic, and cultural policies that make sense to the burning children.[8]

"Theological or otherwise." Greenberg adds that fascinating caveat. He presents us with a near-impossible task at several levels. In the first place, the theological question would forbid the use of God-talk as long as victims continued to be created and would severely limit the amount of God-talk used for comforting victims. It would also limit the victimizers' and victims' uses of God-talk in relation to a past that the abuse of power now overshadows. For example, the theological speech of Jews and Christians after the Holocaust would be limited if either or both communities were creating "burning children" in the present.

In Greenberg's eyes, once suffering enters the picture, language about God can never be spoken with assurance. Whether intentionally or not, he provides an ever-judging, moving criterion for the uses of God in history. Just when judgments can be made and speech about God expanded, a new crisis is bound to confront us. The victims become victimizers so often that the use of suffering as triumphalism threatens to become always the safe harbor for the former victim turned victimizer.

The question remains: What does it mean to be Jewish now? The gaze of burning children calls us to a deeper exploration of our particular identity. The children ask us, above all else, perhaps, to tend to their wounds and to refuse to create another matrix of values that might lead to more burning children. The question of particular identity remains a serious concern for Jews as a primal marker of our being in the world. After these many years of weaving and interweaving possible formulations of Jewish identity within the formative events of our time, the entire search remains foundational both to our sense of outrage and to our hope.

If "Judaism does not equal Israel," what does it equal? Rabbinic Judaism has organized Jewish life for almost two thousand years. Judaism, whatever its religious merits and limitations, has gained a second wind through its allegiance to the Constantinian Jewish establishment. The waves of overt religious renewal issuing from that establishment today, both fundamentalist and progressive, are primarily ways of ordering affluent and powerful individual lives. Thus, the religious settlers in Jerusalem and the West Bank are not so different from the Americans, many of them academics, who form the backbone of these renewal movements. Other dissenters, like Jewish feminists, have also made their peace with the Jewish establishment. Feminism, like other forms of renewal, can be accepted, as long as the centrality of Israel remains in place.

At a time when helicopter gunships painted with the Star of David patrol Palestinian villages, towns, and cities, finding Jewish identity in renewal is insufficient. In any case, its gurus, whether they be the Holocaust theologians or their progressive Jewish counterparts, are aging. Fackenheim has already passed; Rubenstein and Wiesel are in their eighties; Irving Greenberg and the leading figures among progressive Jews, Arthur Waskow and Michael Lerner, are in their sixties and seventies.

Jews of Conscience have been unable to move the process forward in any discernible way. Deep critical thought on the future of Jews and Judaism remains in exile outside these arenas. The Palestinian remnant has its parallel in a Jewish remnant of conscience and steadfastness. The achievements of these remnant Jews and Palestinians are, unfortunately, few and far between. Injustice continues, even as the innocence of Israel is no longer publicly trumpeted. Holocaust theology has lost its creative force; its empty and often simplistic slogans have become enough to insure support for Israel. Overt support among American Jews for Israel wanes, and the dissident Diaspora of individual and small communities of Israelis is increasing. But they have had little if any effect on Israeli policy.

Christian Zionists have added new proponents to the pro-Israel lobby. Many progressive Jews and Christian activists have mounted campaigns against them as unrefined supporters of the state of Israel. These opponents have missed the fact, however, that the pro-Israel narrative now embedded in American foreign policy was developed and enshrined by Jewish and Christian liberals. Some of the neo-conservative political operatives today were liberal in their early days; they continue to argue for Israel using a liberal view of freedom and democracy. From their perspective, protecting Israel upholds individual freedom and economic and political development. Likewise, the political party that could have a more balanced view of the Israeli/Palestinian situation, the Democratic Party, instead vies for the most unbalanced view the Republican Party holds.

The Republicans have been playing catch-up, however, with the Democrats on Middle Eastern issues. For many years the Democrats, partly because of a strong Jewish base, caved in on all things Israel while the Republicans gained no political advantage for doing so. Over the years, their differences have evened out, partly because the Jewish Republican base has increased and partly because accusations of anti-Semitism can cost Republicans legitimacy in the public realm, a vote loser even among non-Jewish voters.

In the end, support for Israel will be found primarily among the elite of Israel and those Israelis who cannot leave the country, the Constantinian Jewish establishment in America, some leftover Christian ecumenical dealers, and Christian evangelicals who identify American power with the coming Kingdom of God. As ordinary Jews absent themselves from this roster, will Constantinian Jews care that they do so?

Jews of Conscience recognize the maps of Israel and Palestine as they are, rather than attempting to transcend and deny them through religious and political rhetoric. In exercising moral conscience, we have been cast adrift. Once the ecumenical deal became a political deal, three mainstream communities—religious Jews, Christians, and American politicians—put Jews of Conscience in a triple bind, excluded by all three groups.

In the 1990s, I thought of how we might bring the Israeli/Palestinian crisis to closure. Closure will not be an ultimate and final justice for either group, but complete justice is an impossibility anyway. The plan began with the acknowledgment that the two peoples are tied together. Since both Palestinians and Jews now share one fate, we must seek to create a shared place where both sides might have room to breathe, a demilitarized space that would grow to involve still more space. If this shared life grew large enough, we could begin to reverse a settler society and end a victimized one. Each entity could call itself what it wanted, and there could also be a name for the new entity to take shape.

The beginning of this shared space would be Jerusalem, the broken middle of Israel and Palestine. History has broken both Jews and Palestinians, and Jerusalem is the middle of that break, geographically as well as culturally, politically, and religiously. The two peoples could meet in Jerusalem, if they could understand that Jerusalem has its own distinctive broken history and that no triumph can be attached to such a difficult history. Acknowledging a broken Jerusalem could forestall exclusive claims on the city from both sides.

Jerusalem could become the beginning of a different map of Jews and Palestinians. As shared space, Jerusalem might return to the ordinary and everyday activities of life within any city. In the movement toward a shared ordinary life, the memory of suffering that each carries in its history could be transformed into a joint memory of possibility and hope. The amazing aspect of Jerusalem would be that ordinary life thrived there; such ordinariness would truly be extraordinary. If Jews and Palestinians shared the responsibilities of an ordinary municipality, from garbage collection to education to policing, a pattern of shared living could be initiated. Palestinians and Jews with children in the same schools would both desire a good education for the children. Living in the same neighborhoods, they would want safe communities. Perhaps, soon, Israelis who longed for security and Palestinians who did not want to be reduced to remnant populations might come to understand that an investment in each other would be the best way of investing in themselves. Over time this model could spread into other areas where Jews and Palestinians lived together. For those who wanted to live separately, that would be fine too.

The question would be whether joint or separate living arrangements were more appealing to the evolving under-standings of both populations. If Jews and Palestinians cre-ated a mixture of joint and separate communities, such an arrangement would suffice. Economic, cultural, and reli-gious mixing might win out in the long run, however, because they would be more dynamic and nourishing. The process would begin with the sharing of Jerusalem as the capital of Is-rael and Palestine and then see where that would lead.

Judaism and Islam, the two majority religious popula-tions of Jerusalem, would also have to partner in establishing common ordinary life. Historically, both religions have an ex-aggerated sense of themselves. They also have been broken by history. Each religion has its own rhythm of power and subjugation; each, its own version of Constantinianism. With Jerusalem demilitarized and filled with ordinary life, Ju-daism and Islam could drop their triumphalism. They might humble themselves before their own people and each other, thereby entering a different phase of their own histories.

The beginning of the journey toward the broken middle of Jerusalem has to begin with confession and an acceptance of what justice is possible. The Palestinians have been driven out of what was Palestine; the Palestinian refugee crisis began with the creation of Israel as a Jewish state. Over time more and more Palestinian land has been taken and settled by Israel. Palestinians would have to accept that movement back to the pre-1948 map of Palestine is impossible.

Israelis and their Jewish enablers in America would have to confess their sins against the Palestinian people. They have been dismissive of Palestinians and Arabs; Palestinians have a right to see Israel and Jews as colonialists and racists. The occupation has never been benign. Jews are not innocent. The confession has to be clear and forthright, made between Jewish and Palestinian leadership in the heart of Jerusalem. The confession must contain a blueprint for the first steps of a new path characterized by equality and shared responsibility. Sharing Jerusalem would be the first step toward a shared land.

Revolutionary forgiveness would begin with confession and resolve in the broken middle of Jerusalem. By revolutionary forgiveness I mean confession that has, at its heart, justice rather than piety. Confession has to be a carrier of change. It must hold an agreement to forge a history different from the past. A mutual path toward justice and equality would bind Jews and Palestinians as recrimination and warfare had joined both in a different way before.

Here is the place where forgiveness enters. Forgiveness comes in the acknowledgment that history is complicated and filled with suffering, and in an agreement to struggle toward a new mutual path. As former enemies enter a new path with justice and equality at the forefront, those who suffered and died to achieve them will not have done so in vain. Even as we mourn the terrible and tragic loss of life and the ethical gutting of traditions and religions, we can say, at least, that

both sides awakened and embraced a different way. With justice on the way, forgiveness is possible, if not for the immediate victims and their families, then for their children and
grandchildren.

Revolutionary forgiveness might look too soft or naive to
offer a solution, but realism and hard politics have not
brought peace. They have, instead, deepened the insecuri-
ties, injustices, and tragedies of the region. The downward
slide began in the 1940s and worsened after the 1967 war.
Jewish thinkers, flush with victory, did not want to think of
any map but our own. Because of the situation in the West
after the Holocaust, the Jewish narrative could be spoken out
loud and with pride for the first time in almost two thousand
years. Who could deny Jews that opportunity? With the wind
finally at our backs, Jews piously and triumphally strutted the
world stage. Hard politics was our new forte.

Within decades of its formation, Israel had become an
imperial power in the Middle East, linked to the United
States. By 1978, Egypt, the major Arab military power, was
safely tucked into the security pocket of the United States.
Israel gained an even freer hand with the Palestinians. With
the fall of the Soviet Union, in the 1980s and 1990s, Arab
governments were deprived of their only patron, and Israel
and the only remaining superpower, the United States, consolidated their regional and global power. By 2000, when the
second uprising began, the Wye map showed a further consolidation and expansion of Israel.

The millions of Israeli-controlled Palestinians were already remnants; they were increasingly isolated and aban-

doned. Every time an uprising or war loomed, the rumor mill about its consequences for these remnant populations began in earnest. The first and second Iraq wars were especially festooned with caution flags. Each might become the opportunity for Israel to solve its demographic "problem" by expelling these remnant Palestinians.

Israel took as much of the land in the West Bank as it could, land with the smallest Palestinian populations, in order to expand its territory and maintain its Jewish majority. Still, in the long run, Israel will have to do something with "their" demographic problem, since whatever happens, Palestinian numbers in Israel keep increasing, far outstripping the growth of the Jewish population. If there is not a movement toward confession and reconciliation, there will come a demographic breaking point, if not in this decade or the next, certainly by midcentury.

The expanding map of Israel forces Palestinians to face various dilemmas. These are dilemmas as opposed to options, since the power equation is so decidedly in Israel's favor. Steadfastness in the land is a dilemma, and it has become almost an empty slogan for Palestinians, who pose it as the only option. Steadfastness in relation to recent defeats can be a form of courage, but it can also become self-defeating. When steadfastness is the only option, even as Israel takes Palestinian territory, the handwriting is on the wall. Over the years, less and less land remains for Palestinians, and with those relentless losses comes the loss of hope.

A political option, soft or hard, becomes a slogan when the reality and the hope are so far removed from each other that what once meant possibility becomes a symbol of despair. The arrival of Ariel Sharon as prime minister in 2000 made clear that the slogans that some Jews and Palestinians held in joint trust, such as "Two states for two peoples," were worse than a false hope.

This false hope of two real and vibrant states has become a fraud. The fraud is simple: there will never be two states, Israel and Palestine side by side, if by Palestine we mean East Jerusalem, the West Bank, and Gaza under full and defensible Palestinian control. This already impossible two-state solution fails to address the return of the Palestinian refugees to their homes and villages in pre-1967 Israel. No reasonable person could hold fast to this solution to the Israeli/Palestinian crisis with the obvious facts on the ground, which can be seen objectively on the maps.

When hopes become empty slogans, a confrontation with reality is at hand. The first and main maneuver is to avoid the confrontation, as the Jewish community in the 1950s tried to avoid confronting the reality of the Holocaust. Those leading the charge against the incorporation of the Holocaust into Jewish life were right in their fear that doing so would change everything. Jewish politics and religion were never the same again. Identity formation shifted precipitately. A new Jew came into being with different interests and attitudes. The formation of this new Jew happened almost overnight. Those who shifted their understandings so clearly and unequivocally bore children into this new identity. For these children and their children, no Jewish identity exists *before* the Holocaust.

In this transformation, Jewish identity took on a violence that it had not previously exercised for at least two millennia. Jews experienced violence when Christians and others perpetrated it against them. Having now assumed political power, Jews became more like their historical Christian neighbors. But to admit this would be to cede the high ethical ground to the Christians who were deep in repentance for the sins of their history. Establishment Jews, rather than cede this ethical ground, used Christian repentance to further Jewish gains in society and the world.

The ethical edge for Jews, held through Christian guilt, whether or not it is warranted, remains crucial to Jewish ascendancy and political power. Israel's case could not be argued without that ethical high ground. It was and is central to the expansion of Jewish power in the United States and Israel. Absent that ground in the court of world opinion, Israel could only be seen in its existence and continuing expansion as a late Western colonial project.

For Jews, identity and covenant are intimately linked. If we deny colonial and racist violence as we embrace it, then, religiously speaking, violence has now entered the very heart of the covenant. Whatever Holocaust theologians have written about God and the covenant after the Holocaust, we are now duly warned that Holocaust theology itself has embedded violence within it. For Palestinians, Israel is a direct negation of what Holocaust theology claims about Jews: that we are innocent and that Israel is part of our redemption. Palestinians who hear the term "Holocaust" must shudder, since it continues to justify actions against them and to cover their continuing displacement.

Israel is not Jewish redemption—even for Israelis. Jews have quite correctly said to Christians: When taken to heart, can Jewish suffering be Christian redemption? The Jewish situation is now parallel. Taken to heart, then, can Palestinian suffering be Jewish redemption? The widening split within Israel between Orthodox Jewish communities and secular Jews has led many of the latter to claim their identity is Israeli, rather than Jewish. Yet now some of those Israelis, especially those who have left Israel because of considerations of conscience, live in the Diaspora. They or their children will be neither Jewish nor Israeli.

This loss of identity leaves us with another quandary. What exactly is an Israeli Diaspora? Israel was to be the solution to the Jewish exile from the land, but now Jews who identify themselves as Israeli are leaving Israel and joining Jews who are Israel-identified but don't want to live in Israel. Other Jews stake their lives on dissenting from Israeli policies. Are these dissidents forming a new Diaspora emerging after the Holocaust and after Israel?

A WOUNDING AMBIVALENCE

Judaism as a religion began as Jews entered a Diaspora situation. More accurately stated, Jews were already in a Diaspora situation when Jerusalem fell, an event that decentered that Diaspora from the Jerusalem Temple and pilgrimages to it.

The "return" to Jerusalem began with the formation of Israel in 1948. It continued after 1967 with the annexation, "unification," and expansion of Jerusalem under Jewish control. This return was supposed to end a Diaspora that many Jews in exile experienced negatively. Jews who first saw Israel as the only place for an authentic Jew to live and who defined Israel as central to Jewish identity, even as they did not live there, hoped that the Diaspora was coming to an end. Some Jews saw Israel as a return to home in their ancient homeland; others felt that the ancient homeland was crucial to the functioning of a vibrant Diaspora that was no longer in exile. With the maps of Israel and Palestine permanent as they are, now the future of Judaism is in question.

Holocaust theology, which saw itself as the natural progression of rabbinic Judaism, never directly addressed what it meant to hold Jerusalem militarily while dispersing a significant part of its indigenous population. Eventually, the Holocaust theologians judged rabbinic Judaism, with its unarmed, stateless Diaspora consciousness, insufficient. It could no longer respond to the urgent questions facing the Jewish people. Religiously, too, rabbinic Judaism was perceived as outdated.

Though God no longer spoke directly to the Jewish people during the Holocaust, the Jewish covenant needed to be reconstructed. The covenant had come into the world at Sinai as a pact between God and the people. Though God had retreated, the Jewish people were called to hold fast to the covenant in the details of Jewish law, Talmudic interpretation, and synagogue prayer. In Greenberg's third era of

Jewish life, as commented and agreed upon by Rubenstein, Fackenheim, and Wiesel, the covenant had been shattered. The only possibility that the covenant might be revived was the return to Jerusalem as the capital of Israel and the center of renewed Jewish life.

The blood and guts of that return to Jerusalem and the creation of Israel as a modern political state are rarely if ever discussed. Why is the "return" to the Land mythologized, and why are those who demythologize Israel shunned and exiled? If rabbinic Judaism or it successor, Holocaust theology, could really stomach the details of power used and abused, it would be better simply to say with Rubenstein that Jews have a necessary power and will use it however we see fit regardless of what other Jews and non-Jews say about it. The Constantinian Jewish establishment could simply say that our redemption was indeed purchased at the expense of the Palestinians and that, in relation to Jews, Palestinians do not count. After all, as the establishment understanding goes, they are uneducated and uncivilized Muslims, Arabs, and Third World people, save for an elite.

Regarding religion and identity, why are Jews unwilling to say that, in the end, we are no better than others who claim their religion or identity as innocent, that Jews and Judaism are no different from Christians and Christianity or Muslims and Islam? When we suffer, like them, we cry suffering. When we have power, like them, we use power while claiming innocence. If Jews are like everyone else, what is the reason to identify as Jewish? Judaism, as a religious identity, neither promises salvation nor has a clear view of the afterlife. For most Jews, God remains an open question, even if they identify Judaism as important to them. Unlike in Christianity and Islam, God is not the sole compelling reason for adhering to Judaism.

Judaism is a religion of doing rather than believing. If the choice is between doing the right and good thing and believing, rabbis counsel doing. Holocaust theologians counsel the same with regard to the state of Israel. Whatever Jews think about God after the Holocaust, the obligation of Jews is to work toward the upbuilding and protection of the state of Israel. Both Fackenheim and Greenberg identified this as a sacred obligation. Whatever arguments theologians like Greenberg put forth—for example, that Jews were going through the difficult process of normalization, where the differences between Jews and others would necessarily diminish—they also argued that some special quality would endure. If that special quality is Jewish ethics, how is this ethics different from that of other communities? Apparently, the difference is based merely on a self-asserted historical claim to chosenness. If it is simply because God chose us from among the nations, what were the parameters of that choice, and were they not dependent on certain actions, especially when we "inherited" the Promised Land?

The image of the Promised Land is another stumbling block. The biblical witness says it was gained through conquest, pillaging, destruction, and rape—often committed in the name of God. Rabbinic Judaism banished or interpreted away this witness. Holocaust theologians do not mention this side of the Hebrew Bible, since they must argue away the violence that befell us and the possible religious reasons for that punishment. The traditional argument for the suffering of God's chosen is that God, as a loving parent, chastises his children in order to bring them back to his fold. Holocaust theologians reject the Holocaust as a punishment for Jewish sins and are bereft of arguments for Jewish suffering. Jewish empowerment is the only answer left to them. Without God in the picture, there could be no judgment on Israel's behavior as it created the Jewish state.

Rabbinic Judaism had no response to the state. This form of Judaism emerged expressly for Jews without a state. Overwhelmed by the Holocaust, Jews, professing Judaism or not, adhered only to the judgments that they themselves could render in relation to the new state. Judgment from outside was hence inadmissible, as was that from Jews of Conscience who spoke up. According to Holocaust theology, the latter must be excommunicated from the Jewish community, seen essentially as non-Jews, part of the Gentile nations.

Holocaust theology continues to rule the Jewish roost even though its original force has dissipated. Even though the actions of Israel, the judgments of Jews of Conscience, and the force of international public opinion ridicule this theology's sense of innocence and redemption in suffering and empowerment, it remains defining. It accepts no divine or human judgment. Nor does it accept a jury of its peers.

The Commanding Voice of Auschwitz, once from the victims, is now its own monopolistic power. Other lessons from the Holocaust, about triumphalism and about the use of the Holocaust against others, are discarded. Perhaps we fear our own inability to define Jewish identity after the Holocaust and after Israel if we face what Holocaust theology and its followers have now rendered.

Where are Jews to go? For Martin Buber and Hannah Arendt, Jews were distinctive, yet small in number; Jews could testify to a world beyond violence partly because of this distinctiveness. A homeland could salvage and present to the Jewish world and others a Jewish positive model in the post–World War II era. However, both saw only danger in the attempt to normalize the Jewish situation through statehood. Statehood would destroy everything. The consequences of the establishment of a Jewish state in Israel, especially the cleansing of large numbers of Palestinians, foretold disaster for both.

The early warnings of Buber and Arendt show how aware they were of the consequences of a politics of dispossession and power enshrined in a modern state. These consequences included the failure of the Jewish ethical tradition, the quashing of internal dissent, and the positing of an exclusive right to narrate a univocal understanding of history, especially a reification of Jew-hatred. In sum, the consequences of statehood would be a disaster for Jews and Arabs. Buber and Arendt came from different angles of vision to the same conclusion. They also shared certain prejudices inherent in their formative years as Jews and Europeans in the twentieth century. Both held a certain sense of chosenness about Jews in general, though they argued that chosenness on quite different grounds. They also shared a sense of Western superiority to the East, which Jews and non-Jews in Europe largely shared.

Their trenchant and laudable analysis of what would befall the Middle East if a Jewish state was established did not overcome their prejudices.

Buber and Arendt shared the Jewish sense of specialness, grounded biblically and then transferred to intellectual capabilities in Enlightenment Europe. Though a sense of specialness can be found in most traditions and communities, they must direct this understanding to the good of the community and others. Buber and Arendt attempted to do this. Yet, perhaps inevitably, specialness morphs into superiority. Some arguments by Buber and Arendt contain notions of superiority toward the Arabs of Palestine and the region. They see Arabs as backward and in need of uplift. Jews can be useful to that uplift, and that can be seen as an argument, if not a justification, for settling a growing number of European Jews in Palestine.

The argument for Jews as the spearhead of European civilization might seem strange in the face of the Nazi debacle at the very heart of European "civilization," the primary victims of which were the Jews of Europe. However, this contradiction shows how deep this current of European superiority ran at the time, essential also to the entire Jewish enterprise in Palestine. Jewish claims of superiority and specialness went beyond constructing a Western-style economy and culture in the land, to an attempt to render Arab culture foreign and a hindrance to the development of "civilization" in the area. These beliefs remain strong today.

Specialness was the underbelly of Jewish analyses of Palestine and Israel. It colored the entire enterprise of state-

hood and the continuing debate about the direction of the Jewish state. In essence, the Jewish sense of specialness and Western superiority, and the Holocaust narrative, have handed Israel the support it needs to pursue ethnic cleansing and occupation without having to state them as policies. In addition, accepted forms of discourse within the Jewish community and in the West allow Israel to deny both policies.

Specialness and superiority have taken on a destructive life of their own since the brakes on Jewish empowerment in Palestine and Israel have been released. If the sense of Jewish particularity had not been so strong and if the Nazis had not risen to power, things might have been different for Judaism. These historical questions are, perhaps, unanswerable. Yet they remain important as we face into the future. Is there a way to negotiate the Jewish narrative that does not limit Palestinians' aspirations and their own sense of destiny? Or does the Jewish narrative have to be abandoned altogether if peace and justice in Israel/Palestine are to be realized?

Emmanuel Levinas was born in Kaunas, Lithuania, lived in France before the Nazi period, and survived there during and after the Nazi years. With Buber and Arendt, Levinas was one of the most significant Jewish philosophers of the twentieth century. Buber and Arendt wrote extensively about Palestine and the state of Israel in direct political terms, arguing for a Jewish community and against a state. Unlike them, Levinas circled these issues, preferring to comment indirectly on the emergence and well-being of the state of Israel.

When I discovered Levinas in the late 1990s, his under-

standing of Jewish life intrigued me, especially his short but powerful evocations of the tasks of the prophets. Yet I also found in him a strange ambivalence, as if there were two parts of him struggling for their own voice. It was as if Levinas was torn asunder by the Jewish witness in the world, the Holocaust, and the state of Israel.

Ostensibly a European philosopher, Levinas was Judeocentric, but his thinking had two sides. The first was strictly European, and he argued his philosophy in those terms; the second was strictly Jewish. In the latter mode, he argued the question of politics and Israel for Jews within a Judaic framework. One might assert that Levinas harmonized in his unique way the two sides that Buber and Arendt argued.

If both Buber and Arendt pioneered Jewish influence on philosophy during the 1960s and 1970s, it can be argued that Levinas did the same in the 1990s and beyond. It is difficult to exaggerate Levinas's influence in academic circles today; yet his Jewish writings and where they lead on the question of Israel are hardly known and rarely analyzed. Levinas shares the same fate as Buber and Arendt on questions that were of great importance to all three as Jews. Levinas yields further questions about how Jews thought, and still think, about Israel, and he may also yield further insight into the path that needs to be pursued in the present. Ambivalent about the emergence of a Jewish state, Levinas was also reluctant to discuss it fully or directly.

The Holocaust and the mass death of Jews were uppermost in Levinas's mind. Yet, Jews were also, or perhaps primarily, a people with a mission before and beyond the state.

The special language of the Judaic was found in sacred texts rather than in territory. Jews guarded these texts, the Torah and the Talmud, and it is here that Jews would find their special destiny and contribute to the world. Nation-states come and go. Moreover, they use violence to survive. Levinas asked whether Israel, the people, should take on the violence of the world.[9]

Levinas was ambivalent about Israel, the state, and the violence of the world it had indeed taken on. On the one hand, Israel, the people, could not help but be affected by the state. On the other hand, who among the nations could or should lecture Israel, the people and the state, about violence? After all, Israel must survive in the world to accomplish its mission. It was that very danger to Israel's existence that made Israel, the state, necessary.

Levinas went back and forth. He warned the people and state of Israel of what was befalling them. He also warned the world to back off; the world, having violated the people Israel for so long, had few moral lessons to communicate. But Levinas explored another, more disturbing understanding grounded in the neighbor, so important to his philosophy. The neighbor was the commanding voice to which and for which the self was responsible, and that voice was primarily Jewish. However, the "Afro-Asiatic," Levinas's term for the Third World, which included Arabs and Palestinians, was not the Jewish neighbor.

In general, Levinas was Eurocentric and identified Jews within that framework. Mostly unsaid but lurking in the background of Levinas's thinking was Israel's fight with the pagan world, now begun again in the Middle East. Salvation came from Europe, the same place that damned the Jews during Levinas's lifetime. Levinas saw the Third World as teeming with the uncivilized hordes waiting to invade the civilized West. Here we find again the irony of Jews seeing the West as civilized and the East as not. Levinas vacillated, catching himself. He sometimes (though not usually) saw Islam as part of the civilized world. Rarely did Levinas see Jews within a global framework. Jewish distinctiveness came within the European framework. He saw Israel, the state, then, within the context of Europe. The reason for its being was Europe. Though inhabiting the land of the Bible, Israel was located in an uncomfortable neighborhood. Its only protection was Europe and a European-oriented state.

In the writings of all these philosophers and theologians, we can see the broad outlines of the problematic of Judaism and Israel. The explosion of Holocaust consciousness and theology made all but invisible the nuances in the thinking of these great—but also limited—Jewish philosophers. The question remains: with the dominance of Holocaust theology, can Martin Buber, Hannah Arendt, and Emmanuel Levinas help move the question of Israel/Palestine forward?

We are, at this moment, in the latest political and ethical bind. The damage of Israel's expansion and seemingly indefinite control of millions of Palestinians is clear and devastating. The Separation Wall is now almost complete. A war in Lebanon was just fought, and others are surely on the horizon.

The homeland vision of Buber and Arendt is past, unfortunately or safely, depending on one's point of view. Also—

unfortunately or safely—Levinas's conflicted sense of the state as needed and as a threat to Jewish ethics also seems past. From another perspective a Jewish homeland in Palestine and ambivalence regarding the state of Israel might be a way of opening up the future of Israel and the Palestinians.

The question of the future is on our doorstep. It is the only relevant question. The Eurocentric hesitations of these Jewish philosophers are a stumbling block. Overcoming that Western bias may be the key to creating a future different from the past. A widely shared understanding in the contemporary Jewish world is that the "Arabs" cannot be trusted and that they represent the modern extension of the anti-Semitic past. The question of Arabs and anti-Semitism is crucial here, having to do with the fear of the Orient and, sad to say, racism toward Middle Eastern peoples.

This racism is backward looking. It carries a Western sensibility toward the East and Arabs that is difficult to justify or explain; it can only be seen as a deeply ingrained prejudice. Add to this prejudice increased Jewish distrust in the wake of the events of September 11 and a new emphasis on Islam as a retrograde force in the world, and the circle of Jewish hesitancy in relation to the Middle East is closed. These great Jewish philosophers mostly ignored Islam, and it played no role in the origins and power of Holocaust theology. This prejudice makes it even more difficult to suggest alternative possibilities for the state of Israel from a Jewish perspective.

The situation of world Jewry for the last two thousand years did not prepare Judaism either for the trauma of the

Holocaust or for the assumption of state power. The warnings of all three philosophers about this unpreparedness went unheeded, and their predictions of the consequences of state power have come true. And more. They also warned that, once assumed, state power would propel Jews into an assimilation to violence and uniformity of thought. This has been achieved in a way approaching totality. Their predictions that this assimilation to state power would marginalize or even criminalize dissent have also come to fruition. However, none of these philosophers predicted the longevity of dissent. The emergence of Jews of Conscience within Israel and the Diaspora has continued and deepened.

Jews of Conscience draw on aspects of these philosophers as well as aspects of Holocaust theology, but we carry these understandings into the twenty-first-century situation of Israel/Palestine. Jews of Conscience have thought through how the two peoples can live together in one area within the context of a transformed relationship. Jews of Conscience are interested in seeing how the divisions created in 1948 and extended ever since can be crossed and healed. Of course, there is never a way back; rather, the question revolves around alternatives for the future. Jews of Conscience seek a secure life for Jews and Palestinians in the Land, one that features justice and reconciliation, equality and, eventually, revolutionary forgiveness.

The prophetic, Buber's indigenous spirituality of the people Israel, must be reembraced. Buber applied that prophetic sensibility to his Jewish homeland, though his Judeocentric, Western prejudice limited his ability to follow this line of thought to the end. Levinas was split on the prophetic. His reliance on the rabbinic as the essence of Judaism tempered his beautiful and compelling writing on the prophetic. Rabbinic Judaism, honed when Jews were outside the Land and existing as minorities in unstable majority situations, limited the prophetic with textual reasoning and legal rulings.

Jews of Conscience must reembrace the prophetic without Judeocentric superiority and rabbinic limitations. This reembracing is impossible within the Jewish establishment today. Thus, we will be exiled from mainstream Judaism. We must also assess whether Israel, the state, can be supported at all within prophetic understandings. If such a state can be supported today, there may yet come a time when it needs to be abandoned. There may need to be a time when we decide that the violence is Israel's and will remain as such. Such a time may come sooner than expected, and if that violence becomes constitutive of the people as well as the state of Israel, Jews of Conscience might have to renounce not only Israel, the state, but also Israel, the people.

The situation worsens daily. The various peace initiatives buy time for Israel's expansion. Peace processes actually facilitate further deterioration of the Palestinian situation. Jews of Conscience in Israel are caught within a state that is deaf to their concerns. State power overpowers their ethical concerns. Jews in the Diaspora continue to speak in the American and European context, but, alas, they too are overpowered by the religious and political discourse that champions Israel against the Palestinians.

Though there has been some modification of the pro-Israel bias in the American media and politics, September 11 and Bush administration policies "corrected" any suspected drift toward Palestinians. The response to former president Jimmy Carter's book, *Palestine: Peace Not Apartheid*, is a case in point. It was released just weeks after the election victory of the Democrats in November 2006; the newly empowered Democratic congressional leaders distanced themselves from Carter in no uncertain terms. They feared declines in funding and punishment from voting blocs, as well as threats to the political support that might catapult them to a decisive victory in the looming presidential election. The subsequent campaign for the presidency also featured a solid pro-Israel consensus. In terms of Israel and the Palestinians there was little or no difference between the Republican and Democratic candidates.[10]

A positive resolution of the Israeli-Palestinian conflict is unlikely in the near future. There are many reasons for this failure. One of them is the Jewish narrative, even as represented by great Jewish philosophers like Buber, Arendt, and Levinas. Their Judeocentric and prejudiced sensibilities limited movement toward a just resolution of the decades-old conflict. Unless Jews of Conscience can move beyond Buber, Arendt, and Levinas, Jews will finally arrive at a situation where there is no moral or viable exit.

5

Prophets in Exile

Surely the prophetic is the greatest Jewish gift to the world. Without the prophetic there is no meaning. The prophetic is not inherited through blood or conferred once and for all. The prophet and the prophetic cannot be institutionalized. Levinas found this independence of the prophet in the Bible, and this independence suggests that prophetic Jews must be politically independent of the Jewish community to be spiritually honest. The prophetic can only be sustained through a life of heartfelt generosity and a practiced critical distance. Neither special privilege nor religious superiority can substitute.

If we are to refuse Hitler, or any tyrant, a posthumous victory, and if we are silent about God unless speaking makes sense in the presence of the burning children, then any political vision can only be a stopgap. Sometimes the Jewish community itself remembers the prophetic or recovers it. Other communities can also sometimes remember and recover it at another time.

Religious statements and hopeful politics lie in a deeper stratum of meaning that is engaged and disengaged simultaneously. Whenever and wherever we are either totally engaged or totally disengaged, we will become stuck in identification and identity, doing violence to ourselves and community and creating the platform from which violence is meted out. We launch a cycle of being violated and violating others. The community that is violated and then violates others is a common enough occurrence in history. When they move toward violence, the people within that community are also violated. If this is the case with Jews today, it is not obvious to whom Jews can turn. If we turn to others, especially those who violated us in the past, there is no guarantee that they won't violate us in the future. The question always before us is how to stop the cycle of atrocities.

Jews as a community often resent and resist the prophetic for the demands it makes upon us, so we should not think that other communities want to live in close proximity to those same demands. The Jewish establishment has always handed over the prophets, except when it could discipline the prophets itself. The prophetic is always seen as subversive of right order and belief. A majority of Jews feel this way; we should expect that Christians and Muslims will feel this way as well.

UN-JEWISH

Once, I showed the Wye maps in a presentation at a community college in Pennsylvania. A young woman in Jewish studies angrily protested that my presentation wasn't Judaic, was "un-Jewish" as she put it. I inquired what she meant. Her response was silence. Then, as I went on to the next raised hand, she stood and stalked out of the room.

Later that evening, I wondered about her comment, her silence, and her abrupt departure. Was the "un-Jewish" element the tone or the facts of my presentation? Perhaps she thought I was only posing as a Jew to present an anti-Judaic lecture. Or perhaps, if she accepted the moral questions the maps raised, she would have to question her own Jewishness.

She had never seen these maps or any others that indicted Jews. She had never heard the suggestion that Jews needed to make a confession to the Palestinian people about what we had done and were doing to them. She referred to Palestinians as "Arabs," a people she may have regarded as beneath an apology from Jews. If, in defending against "them," we had to take an action that, in the best of all worlds, we would never do, how was this defense a wrong in need of confession and apology? From her perspective, I represented the Palestinians, who had to be anti-Semitic because they opposed "our" homecoming in Israel.

Her logic was predictable and pervasive. Jews absolve ourselves by claiming that Palestinians have forced our actions upon us. Their fate is their responsibility, and we bear no culpability. After all, Palestinians always resisted the establishment of Israel, didn't they? And for what reason other than to thwart our homecoming? I saw things another way.

An American-born Palestinian, Souad Dajani, detailed in an e-mail a legal struggle over Jewish land ownership in Israel, land she considers her patrimony:

I haven't bothered to forward info about this because as far as I'm concerned the FACT of Israel is an embodiment of racism. What else would you call a state established on the deliberate ethnic cleansing and dispossession of another people and now claimed to "belong" exclusively to the thieves?[1]

The Jewish studies woman could cite this as another example of anti-Judaic language. Yet if we step back for a moment and listen, doesn't Dajani have a legitimate right to her point of view?

Israel's treatment of Palestinians, with decades of underdevelopment, occupation, invasions, and closures, has left a legacy of food shortages, undependable electricity, and lack of sewage treatment. To the Palestinian author of yet another article on Gaza in December 2007, detailing the extreme deprivation of an ordinary day, I wrote:

> Mr. Sami Abdel Shafi,
>
> I was just forwarded an article you wrote on your experiences in Gaza. I am simply writing to tell you how meaningful your words are and how tragic the situation is that they describe. I am a Jewish-American who is finishing yet another book on the Israeli-Palestinian "crisis." It is so clear that I with others have failed miserably in addressing and changing your life situation.[2]

The horror of it all is contained in the phrase I used in my writing, "Israel proper." Is Israel proper the one according to the maps of 1948, 1967, 1999, or today? "Failing miserably" is hardly enough to say. I used human rights language, which is fine for progressive Jews but fails to address political rights. Where do Ms. Dajani's and Mr. Abdel Shafi's political rights and the political rights of Jews begin and where do they end?

Jews can discuss our rights based on the Warsaw Ghetto during the Nazi era. Without having known at that time where the ghettoization would lead, and without making any predictions about where present-day ghettos might lead, we can see the human and political rights that the Jews of Warsaw needed. There was no excuse for depriving Jews of those rights. What did Jews have the right to expect from the surrounding community in their dire need? And what words and actions, if any had been offered, would have been sufficient from the perspective of a Jew in the ghetto? One person alone cannot change an entire political situation, but we have personal responsibilities, whatever effect they may or may not have. Jews have judged severely the Polish Christians' lack of words and actions. Perhaps we can now accept that power brings excuses and a false feeling of powerlessness that can be morally judged.

Dajani circulated another article on "waterboarding," the much-discussed American torture tactic of choice after September 11. To it she appended another "anti-Judaic" comment:

This was also featured on TV recently. I was struck by the CIA guy who said he was so angry after 9-11 and wanted to do whatever it took. Sure he was

angry. But would we allow the same emotions to
people whose families the US is now crushing and
killing in Iraq and Afghanistan? To the victims of our
"ally"—Israel's—devastating siege of Gaza? To the
families of over 30 Palestinians who died because
Israel wouldn't let them seek out medical care? To
the families of Iraqi kids dead and dying under US
occupation?[3]

No doubt to the minds of many, Dajani is relentless and
ties everything to Israel, like a giant circle that keeps coming
back to her touchstone, Palestine. Her obsession with it is so
akin to our fixation on the Holocaust and Israel that it infuri-
ates Jews even more. When the image in the mirror is one
you don't want to see, it is easier to curse the Palestinian mirror than to see the reflected image. In the Jewish mirror is
the reflected image of an accusation we once lodged against
others.

Palestinians have become our interlocutors and prophets. Like the prophets of old and Jews of Conscience today,
they emerge from within Israel itself. When these prophets
confront us, they bring us face-to-face with the other half of
the Jew within, the part the Jewish community seeks to deny.
The Palestinians, in solidarity with Jews of Conscience, offer
a way toward healing that Jews have wanted, needed, and rejected since the Holocaust.

The Palestinian other has become stronger within the
Jewish world as more and more Jews of Conscience have become other to mainstream Jewish life. The disturbing force

of these others is now permanently embedded within Jewish history. We don't need Freud to understand that we seek to banish the other because it is too close to us, and even without Jung, we know that we have to deny our shadow. We try to keep the Palestinian other out precisely because it touches the deepest root of our Jewishness.

The other offers us *teshuvah*, a turning that is repentance. The turning itself is movement within; it is facing who we are and who we have become. The place from which we have turned away, we must now turn toward. Turning is psychological and spiritual. In Jewish life, however, it is also moral. It is bound up with the prophetic, a simultaneous hearing and practice of the prophetic. The prophetic cannot be only inward. The prophetic has always come from the margins, the widow, the orphan, and the poor—the individuals the established do not want to become. Palestinian widows, orphans, and poor cannot be safely tucked behind the wall that Israel has built. They will not disappear, and our rhetoric of anti-Semitism and terrorism cannot drown them out. The prophetic call will not dissipate because we define and dismiss them as uncivilized, stupid, or immoral.

The prophets emerged exactly for such others. In the beginning, the ancient Israelites were the other. The Pharaoh and the entire Egyptian royal establishment viewed them in the same pejorative way as Jews view Palestinians. In Egypt, the Israelites and other slaves dwelling in the land became the other within. The Egyptian empire was built on oppressing and silencing its subject peoples; it was for these oppressed and silenced that God spoke. God chose Israelites with internal access to Pharaoh's palace to speak to that power system, which could not listen. Then the enslaved left to be on their own, with their own God. As it turned out, the escape from slavery and into freedom became a supreme ordeal before the Israelites reached the Promised Land. Then another ordeal, as intense as the wandering, began.

In the Torah, and later with the Writings and the Prophets, there is no conclusion to this cycle of promise and ordeal. Alternating between hope and despair, between peace and war, and between justice and expulsion, we are left, finally, without an end. The founding of the people Israel, with all of its back and forth, will continue, a destiny perpetually played out in the world.

In the Bible, Israel past will be forever Israel, as long as God doesn't change his mind, which has happened on more than one occasion. Israel carries an anxiety that the chosen people will be abandoned. The prophets announce the word of an angry and vacillating God who will expel them. God and the prophets, however, only call Israel's bluff. It is Israel that vacillates. Israel abandons its own charge; Israel betrays its own mission; Israel turns against its own indigenous prophetic, a turning away that the Bible identifies as idolatry. Each betrayal and act of idolatry results in a new dispersion.

The assertion of a fixed Jewish identity is idolatry. Israel originated as a number of tribes that became a people, but each tribe had its own indigenous history and traditions. The Bible describes the Israel that left Egypt in a variety of ways, among them as a "mixed multitude." Once in the Promised Land, they mixed with Canaanites and others, already there, who were also themselves mixed. Thus mixtures are the origins of the people Israel. The objections of today's Constantinian Jewish establishment to intermarriage and assimilation are older than Judaism itself, and predate the formation of Israel; Israel as a people was impossible without racial, cultural, political, national, and religious mixing. Without mixing, it is impossible today.

Over time, mixture becomes fusion, and an assortment blends in a process sometimes easy, other times difficult. Combining elements of culture and religion into identities goes on and on endlessly. Identities that are named, especially religious identities—Jew, Christian, Muslim—may seem solid, as if they remain continuous with and like their ancient forms. Yet all religious identities are partly invented and constantly changing, including, of course, Jewish identity.

Jewish identity has changed many times. Greenberg's understanding of three eras of Jewish history is helpful but understated. The late Efraim Shmueli, an Israeli historian, divided Jewish history into eight eras. He asserted that each era was so different that we should rethink the assumption that a Jew from one era could recognize a Jew from another era as a Jew. In Shmueli's view, Jews understanding each other across eras is highly unlikely.[4]

When we add the periodic breakdown, transformation, and re-reification of religious identities, identity politics, so rampant in the world, seems risky. Risk augurs caution. We should be especially cautious about identity politics when the power of constructed and assumed identities becomes power in the world. The fourth era of Jewish life, Constantinian Judaism, cannot define Jews and Judaism forever. The first two eras of Jewish life were marked by a thousand-year difference. The third era of Jewish history lasted only decades. The Constantinian Era may be fated to last only that long. We are perhaps at the terminus of Jewish history, one that will keep Constantinian Judaism alive by sheer power, but with fewer and fewer Jews involved in it.

Despite the steady drumbeat of the Holocaust and Israel, there are many signs that ordinary Jews in Israel and America have ceased to listen to the Constantinian Jewish establishment. Over time the rank and file will find another outlet for their pursuits and loyalties. Their children will encounter such hollowness at the core of Jewish identity that their distance from things Jewish will increase until, incrementally, the core disappears. Unless another unifying element emerges, Jewish affiliation may dwindle to the point of no return.

Jewish leadership has brought us to where we are today, with a state and hyperpower. Coupled with the resentment that has been building against the Jewish exercise of power over the years, including among the partners in the ecumenical deal, a sudden collapse of Jewish power might indeed ignite a backlash against Jews. Jews might already be in a Catch-22 situation where only more power will secure the Jewish future, and Jews of Conscience may be as exposed as we have ever been. In the end, however, power over others is impossible to maintain and extend forever. It simply delays the day of reckoning and makes the fall even more precipitate.

In the Holocaust, the Nazis forced the identity "Jew"

upon diverse millions from different cultures, language groups, and histories. Though it was true that most self-identified as Jews, that one marker hid the incredible diversity that existed beneath the marker. This identity marker was limited to European Jews, who were a significant catalog of "Jews" in the world, but by no means definitive or exhaustive.

Jews often mistake, limit, and demarcate "Jew" as primarily or exclusively belonging to their group of Jews. By and large, European Jews believed that their Jewishness was the only authentic Jewishness in the world. That is why, when referring to the state of Israel of the 1950s and beyond, Jews from Arab and North African backgrounds in Israel were routinely and forcibly "educated" into the "real" Jewish identity of the dominant European Jewish elite. Israeli and American Jews assert that tradition today by assuming these communities define "authentic" Jewish identity and Jewish religiosity, delimiting any Jewishness and Judaism outside the parameters they define.

When I have felt less Jewish than someone else, wanted to distance myself from Judaism, felt Jewishness leaving me, or have been defined as not Jewish, I have experienced another form of Jewishness, one that existed in history and is now forgotten. I am also part of a Jewishness that has yet to emerge. With other Jews, I am part of yet another transformation of Jewishness that might help give birth to a new era of Jewish life after the Holocaust and after Israel.

Making the rounds in, Jewishly speaking, out-of-the-way places over the years, I have heard the rumblings of a profound discontent about Israel. Whether one wants to attribute these to the old or the new anti-Semitism, and whether they are rational or irrational, will matter little when the power game shifts. This growing discontent may be why the Jewish establishment has embraced Christian Zionist movements. They differ with most Jews on every part of the Jewish liberal agenda save Israel, and their view of saving Israel is to let it be destroyed in the here and now. Their apocalyptic vision wants to save Israel by losing it and to save Jews from Judaism by converting us. Greenberg's permanent interests rather than permanent friends may deliver us into the hands of these born-again Christians.

THE MEZUZAH ON OUR DOORPOST

Levinas once described how, in the wake of the 1967 war, the "young uprooted themselves and went to live in Israel." A home so sure of its inhabitants' identity can send its uprooted young out, fed on the ideas and hopes of the world. Such youth are "ready to sacrifice themselves for an idea . . . are capable, in other words, of extremist ideas." Those days are behind us. The mythology that erupted around the Holocaust and Israel is gone; it will never be recovered. Quite the opposite. Both are receding, becoming more and more distant, their veil lifted.[5]

Levinas warned that there were many Jews who were living in houses without a mezuzah at the door. They were absent of any sign of the core commitment to God who relativizes all human powers. Such a house "exists as an abstract space traversed by the ideas and hopes of the world.

Nothing can halt them, for nothing hails them." Then: "Inte-
riority's act of withdrawal is undone before their unstoppable
force. The Judaism of the Diaspora no longer has an interior.
It enters deeply into a world to which it is nonetheless opposed. Or is it?"[6]

How grating it is to read this essay, especially now that
mezuzot are found on the doorposts of Jewish homes everywhere. What does a home laden with mezuzot mean, if they
are signs of violence against others, Palestinians and Jews of
Conscience? Modern Judaism, with its mezuzot, has taken
on the full force of the violence that Levinas warned against
and was himself ambivalent toward.

Building one's future on power that could inflict violence
so as not to suffer at the hands of violence again was understandable. After suffering violence and perpetrating it, being
completely without power would be suicidal. The Jewish
community is divided between Constantinian Jews and Jews
of Conscience. Perhaps each has its own function, one holding down the fort of empire, the other exploring a new
wilderness of community.

When I teach the Holocaust, my Christian students are
aghast at what Christians have done to Jews. Could these
possibly have been Christians? Their answer is decidedly
not, whatever they claimed. They disavow such acts as Christian. But, of course, the perpetrators were Christians, and
truly so, as are the Jews who cleanse Palestinians from the
Land. The Jews who argue special privilege and racial superiority are in denial as they destroy Palestinians' homes and
build their own on the footprint of the homes just destroyed.

Without missing a beat, these mezuzah-bearing Jews are just like the Christians who so easily brandished the cross.

History sneaks up on the powerful. The judgment of history arrives when an ideology is so demythologized that it has less and less capacity to inspire the public. Then the powerful must instill the mythology in the public consciousness with grand public monuments that command attention. In the beginning the public is drawn to these monuments; over time their meaning has to be explained and commanded. The mass killing of Jews in Europe became the Holocaust became the Holocaust Memorial Museum became the mandate of teaching the Holocaust in school curricula. By the time Christian students reach my university Holocaust class, they have read Elie Wiesel's *Night* at least once, often twice, sometimes three times.

Yet these Christian students are unprepared for the journey through their own history. The monumentalized and museumed Holocaust ironically becomes a safe harbor for them. The Holocaust has become suffering that can be embraced with a happy ending. They can empathetically join suffering Jews without having to face the difficult questions arising from their own tradition.

Since the Holocaust has become a safe harbor for Jews as well, should I object to my students' resistance to discussions about evil that was signed with the cross? We have come to a time where the Holocaust is romanticized and used for so many issues and feelings that perhaps we should let it function for whomever in whatever way it works for them. If we disturb their rendition, we would also have to disturb our own.

Disturbing everyone means freeing the Holocaust to cease to be The Holocaust. At least, it should cease to be The Holocaust that justifies the suffering of others. But, again, what would we be as Jews if the Holocaust is not enshrined in museums that we are supposed to visit and repeated in slogans we are supposed to mouth? Perhaps we could become Jews who hailed ideas and hopes that shelter Palestinians under the sign of the mezuzah rather than expelling them in its name.

The posting of the mezuzah, a commandment, has many different interpretations. We have choices: the mezuzah as a sign of violence or the mezuzah as a sign of solidarity, the mezuzah as a sign of distance from the other or the mezuzah as a sign of embrace. The mezuzah is a sign of protection through power, and it is a sign of healing through suffering. The mezuzah means we belong as Jews. The mezuzah is, too, a sign of Jewish exile. The mezuzah means all these and more. Is the commandment fulfilled in our time by the mezuzah that hails the 614th or the 615th commandment? Since both commandments are there, already presented to the Jewish community, we face the challenge of how to embrace both, thereby refusing Hitler a posthumous victory and refusing to denigrate the Palestinian people.

THE PROPHETIC WILD CARD

The majority of Jews are busy making a living and trying to make sense of their own lives, as every community does. More or less without an agenda, and uninvolved in the civil war between Constantinian Jews and Jews of Conscience, they are left to fend for themselves whatever comes their way.

In the main, Constantinian Jews are a wealthy and connected minority, and progressive Jews, the left wing of Constantinian Judaism, share its power, albeit in somewhat different circles. Strategy doomed Jewish progressives, demanding a fold here and a tuck there, forcing them to condemn other Jews to the left of them, even as they were being accused by the Constantinian establishment of being disingenuous and hiding their real intentions. The Constantinian establishment was no doubt correct, though this was a case of the pot calling the kettle black. The powers that be disguise their control behind the cloak of innocence and redemption. Progressive Jews disguise their acquiescence in power by pretending resistance. Jews of Conscience offer a wild card in the pretend civil war between Constantinian and progressive Jews.

Jewish history cannot account for the destiny that the prophetic wild card has laid upon it. The Jews of certain status labor incessantly to bury the prophetic, but in the end they will fail. Where the prophetic comes from or why it erupts is mysterious. The prophet often also does not know. If prophets knew the where and why of the prophetic, they might choose to deflect or bury a call so disruptive and disturbing. Probing the wound and trauma to discover the meaning of Jewish identity can seem extreme. Indeed, it is. The prophets are an unruly, uncompromising bunch. Even if they come from power, having received their prophetic commission, they are soon on the road. That road is often one of hot pursuit; the powerful hunt the prophets because they announce the violation of the covenant and its exclusion in the precincts of power.

There are some who believe that Israel was chosen precisely because it was on the margins of Egyptian society. In the Biblical Era, the covenant traveled with the Israelites. If the covenant, once given, travels throughout history, it cannot be restricted to Jews and the Jewish people. God surely is with those on the outside. The covenant is wherever there is need and want. This means, on the one hand, that no community has an exclusive grasp on the covenant, that no special privilege is attached to the covenant. On the other hand, those who search for the covenant must move among those on the margins in order to be part of it.

The Jewish question now is why the covenant has deserted us in our abuse of power and where we might find it again. It might still be that the covenant Holocaust theologians thought was discarded and broken is alive and well. Since the prophetic emerges from a zone that is impossible to quantify, harboring within it a power that challenges injustice in odd and baffling ways, is it possible that the prophetic signals a need to once again pay attention to God.

The prophetic after the Holocaust and after Israel is not the same as the prophetic of ancient Israel. It is relevant to each era into which it erupts. Shmueli in arguing his eight cultures of Jewish history notes that the continuity within the discontinuity revolves around God, Torah, and the Land. What he fails to mention is the link among all three—the prophetic. It is the prophetic that places all three into motion, defines and redefines them in each Jewish culture, and surprises all of them.

All cultures attempt to domesticate the prophetic to establish stability. The prophetic, as the wild card, emerges at a moment's notice, on its own time. It is emerging again now with Jews of Conscience, and not surprisingly, these Jews are found wherever the maps of injustice exist around the world.

In exile, Jews of Conscience have joined a new Diaspora, where exiles from all over the world and from different cultures, traditions, and religions find their home together. The rebirth of the Jewish prophetic is happening in the hinterlands of Jewish power and status. Thus we are in and outside of Jewish life, which gives us a fulcrum to generate a different prophetic energy requisite to the times in which we live. We are involved in global struggles with others, including non-Jews, in the difficult attempt to birth a new political and economic world order.

Mourning for the Future

Jamie Kastner, a Toronto filmmaker, created the documentary road movie *Kikes Like Me*. Kastner, who never offers us his ethnic and religious affiliation in the film, travels the world—New York, London, Jerusalem, Paris, and Berlin—"being" Jewish and asking a variety of folks what being Jewish means to them. He finds that the word "Jewish" carries much negative baggage. At first, Kastner greets this negativity with light humor. As Auschwitz comes closer, Kastner's tone changes. One reviewer noted:

> By the time Kastner's journey reaches Auschwitz, his early gentle sarcasm has hardened at every stop and a burning influx of anger gives his words as much heat as the dutifully restored ovens in their prime. The brilliance of this fascinating chronicle is that by the end of the trail, it matters not a wit who's Jewish and who isn't. Untested assumptions will continue to poison the planet: ignorance is a much deadlier enemy than any race, colour or creed.[1]

Felicia Lee, a *New York Times* reviewer, also drew attention to Kastner's depiction of Auschwitz: his tone darkens as the road trip ends at the concentration camp museum at Auschwitz. Mr. Kastner wonders if the museum bar serves Manischewitz wine and angrily mutters: "It's strange to have it preserved here like some kind of movie set for our benefit," observing the tourists eating as they wander among the death ovens.[2]

The Jewish period of mourning the dead, extensive in the first days, is then marked yearly. The dead are remembered as an affirmation of life and its continuation. Death is to be contemplated within the framework of life. That is why the Kaddish, the Jewish prayer over the dead, never mentions death. The Kaddish does speak confidently of the coming Kingdom of God. Since the prayer developed during the Rabbinic Era, when God had ceased to speak, it is perhaps the Jewish retort to a silent God—we as Jews will speak to God even though God has ceased speaking to us. We will keep up our end of the covenant even if God hasn't. The Kaddish is a prayer of hope; it can also be understood as a prayer of defiance.

Kastner takes a journey of affirmation. His journey, like the Kaddish, is also a journey of defiance. This is what it has come to, tourists eating as they tour death. But what does one do when death is a tourist attraction? If close to a million people a year visit Auschwitz, everything needed at any tour site is there. This includes food and bathrooms and maintenance crews and security, with parking for large tour buses and medical facilities for those who need aid.

Do people fall ill from the death or the food? Medically speaking, it matters. The physician needs to know what to prescribe for the ailment. Theologically speaking, it matters as well. If physical illness at Auschwitz strikes because of death rather than food, the remedy lies somewhere else than modern medicine. The remedy is some kind of activity that bespeaks a healing, a mourning that spurs activity to further life. That activity has to be as deep as the death witnessed. It cannot rest within the acceptable, since the acceptable now is often the demise of others. The tourism that defines Auschwitz today must be struggled against—outside of Auschwitz.

For some Jews of Conscience and Palestinians the struggle ahead is for a shared life in one state, rather than the much discussed, delayed, and now virtually impossible two-state option. Just days after the Annapolis gathering, a group of dissident Israelis and Palestinians issued "The One State Declaration." A warning is in order. The declaration is direct, with harsh indictments and language. For those learned in the language of diplomacy, the declaration crosses many sacred boundaries. Yet for the untrained mind, the declaration may make obvious sense. Who would want to deny Israelis and Palestinians a shared and just future?

> For decades, efforts to bring about a two-state solution in historic Palestine have failed to provide justice and peace for the Palestinian and Israeli Jewish peoples, or to offer a genuine process leading towards them.
>
> The two-state solution ignores the physical and political realities on the ground, and presumes a

false parity in power and moral claims between a colonized and occupied people on the one hand and a colonizing state and military occupier on the other. It is predicated on the unjust premise that peace can be achieved by granting limited national rights to Palestinians living in the areas occupied in 1967, while denying the rights of Palestinians inside the 1948 borders and in the Diaspora. Thus, the two-state solution condemns Palestinian citizens of Israel to permanent second-class status within their homeland, in a racist state that denies their rights by enacting laws that privilege Jews constitutionally, legally, politically, socially and culturally. Moreover, the two-state solution denies Palestinian refugees their internationally recognized right of return.

The two-state solution entrenches and formalizes a policy of unequal separation on a land that has become ever more integrated territorially and economically. All the international efforts to implement a two-state solution cannot conceal the fact that a Palestinian state is not viable, and that Palestinian and Israeli Jewish independence in separate states cannot resolve fundamental injustices, the acknowledgment and redress of which are at the core of any just solution.

In light of these stark realities, we affirm our commitment to a democratic solution that will offer a just, and thus enduring, peace in a single state based on the following principles:

- The historic land of Palestine belongs to all who live in it and to those who were expelled or exiled from it since 1948, regardless of religion, ethnicity, national origin or current citizenship status;
- Any system of government must be founded on the principle of equality in civil, political, social and cultural rights for all citizens. Power must be exercised with rigorous impartiality on behalf of all people in the diversity of their identities;
- There must be just redress for the devastating effects of decades of Zionist colonization in the pre- and post-state period, including the abrogation of all laws, and ending all policies, practices and systems of military and civil control that oppress and discriminate on the basis of ethnicity, religion or national origin;
- The recognition of the diverse character of the society, encompassing distinct religious, linguistic and cultural traditions, and national experiences;
- The creation of a non-sectarian state that does not privilege the rights of one ethnic or religious group over another and that respects the separation of state from all organized religion;
- The implementation of the Right of Return for Palestinian refugees in accordance with UN Resolution 194 is a fundamental requirement for justice, and a benchmark of the respect for equality;
- The creation of a transparent and non-discriminatory immigration policy;

- The recognition of the historic connections between the diverse communities inside the new,
  democratic state and their respective fellow communities outside;
- In articulating the specific contours of such a solution, those who have been historically excluded
  from decision-making—especially the Palestinian
  Diaspora and its refugees, and Palestinians inside
  Israel—must play a central role;
- The establishment of legal and institutional
  frameworks for justice and reconciliation.

The struggle for justice and liberation must be
accompanied by a clear, compelling and moral vision
of the destination, a solution in which all people who
share a belief in equality can see a future for themselves and others. We call for the widest possible discussion, research and action to advance a unitary,
democratic solution and bring it to fruition.[3]

Among the signatories of the declaration was Ilan Pappe, one
of the new Israeli historians. After publishing his book *The
Ethnic Cleansing of Palestine*, Pappe left Israel, or Palestine,
for Exeter University in the United Kingdom. By leaving,
Pappe, like Kastner, raised vexing questions about Jewish
identity. Sixty years after the founding of Israel, the question
of Jewish identity is a hot topic, for Jews and for others. Jewish identity now seems in perpetual crisis.

With so many intricate issues and radical concerns on the
table sixty-plus years after Auschwitz and the founding of the

state of Israel, Jewish identity is now endangered. In the first place, it is crystal clear that we as Jews have come to the end of the Jewish history we have known and inherited. Making ethical claims about the Jewish tradition in relation to other communities is no longer possible. Whether in fact Jews historically ever had an ethical edge is open to dispute. What Jews did have was the claim they made. This claim helped us through difficult and dark periods. With this ethical claim our history could be seen through the lenses of innocent suffering and divinely mandated, innocent empowerment. That claim is now unavailable—even as we need it more than ever.

In the second place, though our power can be and sometimes is exaggerated, to deny it is ridiculous. Israel is the dominant military power in the Middle East, joined at the hip to the only superpower in the world, the United States. In the United States, Jewish influence is everywhere. Often used for good, it is also used to stifle dissent and orient intellectual and political life toward Jewish interests as defined by the Jewish establishment. Whether the Jewish establishment actually advances Jewish interests in the long run is highly debatable. Regardless, Jewish power is in every nook and around every corner in America. Any Jewish dissident knows this on a visceral and experiential level. Non-Jews who speak on behalf of Palestinians know this as well.

In the third place, the religious and political landscape for Jews changed forever when the ecumenical dialogue became the ecumenical deal, and this deal, in turn, became the political deal. This deal pretends Jews are innocent and any criticism of Israel is anti-Semitism. Whether the traditional or the new anti-Semitism card is played, a statute of limitations seems on the brink of being invoked.

The distinction between real Jew-hatred and political gamesmanship is becoming increasingly blurred. To see the Palestinians as Jew haters is to characterize political disputes in nonnegotiable terms. The accusation of anti-Semitism is thus used as an avoidance mechanism that seeks to deflect challenges to Jewish power when such challenges are understandable and legitimate.

Maturity is the ability to separate anti-Semitism and political differences. After September 11, non-Jews and some Jews became more aware of the need to differentiate political differences and Jew-hatred. If Jews have indeed reentered history as a power to be reckoned with, there will be those who need and want to reckon with that power. Politics is a power game. Jews are not exempt. Those who benefit from Jewish power will welcome it, and those who are injured by that power will oppose it.

This separation leads us to a fourth consideration. Anti-Semitism is real. Jews born after the Holocaust and the formation of the state of Israel do not know what it is like to live without either formative event at the center of our identity. Even though in my lifetime, the Holocaust and Israel were not always the center of Jewish identity, there is little use denying that both are now central. Clearly Jews have suffered enormously and Jews still need empowerment. The point is less to reverse the direction of Jews toward empowerment than it is to use whatever power we have to move toward an interdependent empowerment with others.

Jews are more secure when our flourishing is tied to the flourishing of others. There will always be movements that seek unilateral power. Such movements have been and will continue to be ominous for everyone; they are particularly bad for Jews. The idea that a small minority of Jews in the United States and small nation in the Middle East can go it alone or tied only to the United States is a myth that ought to be demystified along with the other mythology that prevents Jewish self-analysis of our place and future in the world.

Fifth, though the separation of Jews into three groups, Constantinian Jews, progressive Jews, and Jews of Conscience, is highlighted today, there is a fluidity here that might move certain numbers of Jews out of one category into another. What seems definitive today can change tomorrow. What is certain is that Jews of Conscience provide the ethical witness necessary to continue with Jewish life.

In the main, Jews are a doing/thinking people, spurred by the indigenous prophetic. Jewish rituals and identity markers have always been secondary to textual analysis and reasoned debate, even in the Rabbinic Era. The biblical witness is even more startling in its critique of false religion. Jews who feast off of empire and enable its growth for the benefit of themselves will be judged as the Israelites were: by the proliferation of widows, orphans, and the poor.

The role of conscience is of utmost importance. Whenever tradition and assertion of power are confronted by conscience, conscience calls both to account. Movements of Jewish renewal that operate as the left wing of Constantinian Judaism create and enforce the parameters of acceptable dissent, inhibiting radical Jewish thought and action. This thought and action are precisely what Jews need if we are going to face the fact of who we have become.

The sixth understanding is the need for the rebirth of the prophetic. Though indigenous to the people Israel, the prophetic, like the covenant, travels. The covenant cannot be equated with injustice. Injustice practiced over a sustained period of time leaves the community without the covenant. Though the community claims the covenant, hoping that the claim itself will protect the community from scrutiny, the reality is that the covenant travels to those on the margins.

The right of the weak and oppressed to that claim is indisputable. The covenant, already in history and disposed toward those on the margins, can be found there. The covenant can be practiced without a sure sense of God and even as a protest against the absence of God because the pursuit of justice and its absence are more important than belief in God. The struggle for justice demythologizes God and the people who claim God as their legitimacy. The refusal to practice idolatry is always and everywhere better than singing God's praises while making God an enabler of injustice.

The seventh consideration is what must be done in relation to the state of Israel. The questions that Jews of Conscience bring to bear on the origins of Israel and its permanent expansion cannot be trumped by previous thought or recede in the face of the need to continue to support Israel only because of the fear of what the withdrawal of support might mean to the Jewish inhabitants of Israel. The "One State Declaration" says that the "two-state solution entrenches and formalizes a policy of unequal separation on a land that has become ever more integrated territorially and economically" and that "[a]ll the international efforts to implement a two-state solution, as unlikely as that is, cannot conceal the fact that a Palestinian state is not viable, and that Palestinian and Israeli Jewish independence in separate states cannot resolve fundamental injustices." These assertions mean that redress is "at the core of any just solution." If we agree that the two-state solution does not create two equal states, that it does not grant adequate rights to Palestinians, and that it uses false premises to create peace, should we conclude that the two-state solution is ethically wrong?

The declaration adds that the two-state solution "condemns Palestinian citizens of Israel to permanent second-class status within their homeland, in a state that denies their rights by enacting laws that privilege Jews constitutionally, legally, politically, socially and culturally," all the while denying Palestinian refugees their "internationally recognized right of return." Israel has also conquered Jerusalem and the West Bank and has a permanent occupation within and around the second remnant of the Palestinian people, which means that Israel has effectively made the territory between Tel Aviv and the Jordan River one state. Unless Israel reverses its course, there can be no way forward that is honest without affirming and working toward justice within that one state.

It is extremely unlikely that Israel will reverse its expansionist course. Does this political standstill condemn Jews of Conscience to support what Constantinian and progressive

Jews support, albeit without the patronizing and demeaning discussions surrounding the intractable issues? Jewish dissent may be fated to become a footnote to a policy that won't be reversed, but at least we can say that there were Jews who said no, at least theoretically.

Jews of Conscience seem caught here. There is a permanent occupation of Jerusalem and the West Bank. There will not be two states in any real sense of that term, only one state, which Israeli power established, with millions of Palestinians within it. One state will not be officially declared—it will be de facto; to declare it would end the Jewish state idea without which Jews would leave Israel and probably would not survive their changed status, in the present atmosphere at least. Nonetheless, the Constantinian Jewish support for Israel's expansionistic objectives has already passed its time. Constantinian power will accomplish many of its goals, among them the severe diminishment of Palestine. The progressive Jewish two-state option is too limited, has become dishonest, and is discredited—it is simply a cover for power. Jews of Conscience will also lose. A single state is not going to happen, whatever is wanted or needed.

Before a more general wasteland comes into being, the Palestinians will already have been wasted. Something will have to be done to the restive and growing Palestinian remnants—and soon. Integration is one possibility, but neither Constantinian nor progressive Jews hope for this, so they are not willing to work toward this goal. Without predicting what will happen to the Palestinian population centers over the long run, it is probably best to think the opposite of inclusion.

Can Jews of Conscience protect Palestinians, or Israelis for that matter, from the fate that seems inevitable?

What is did not have to be; there were other choices. Yet the choices made, so determinative of the present, can be altered if the will is there. The wasteland of today—the center of the struggle to be faithful—can become the prospect for a future beyond desolation. Jews of Conscience especially are called to disentangle themselves from the inevitable sweep of history, if only to see clearly and to place before the community another possible future.

This time we are aware that there is no homecoming that can be celebrated at the expense of the other. When one community's redemption means the suffering of another, it cannot be redemption for either. Christians have learned this; now we as Jews have. Can Muslims be far behind?

Mourning together, we begin to piece together another way. The prophetic is exiled; the exile is prophetic. That the best view is from exile is lamentable but again so Jewish. Next to the prophetic, exile is the most practiced of the primal Jewish identities. Perhaps they are tied together again, the prophetic and exile, as they were at the beginning of Jewish history. Perhaps the prophetic will always be in exile. Does that mean that God will always be in exile too?

Joan Casanas, a Spanish priest, wrote that God does not exist without justice. If this axiom is taken to its logical conclusion, God might never exist. Like Greenberg's burning children, the question of God made too difficult might throw us off track—like affirming God too easily.

The way forward cannot be discerned using only the

question of God's presence or absence. Judaism and Jewishness can move forward only with the doing of justice, even when the acts committed seem un-Jewish. How else to break the cycle of violence and atrocity committed in God's name and our own? What will happen in the future is beyond our capacity to imagine or produce. By definition that is left to the next generation.

Mourning and lament are our final say to the future. Isn't this also the sign of the greatest hope? In that hope God returns. Or doesn't. God waits for us or we wait for God. Have God and the human ever been in perfect sync? Doing what we can, we testify for ourselves and for God. It is our responsibility, our obligation. It is what we are called to be. What God is about, when God will speak, and what God will say are beyond our power. Perhaps beyond our imagination.

That the Jewish testimony in the world needs renewal is beyond questioning. Its importance is also beyond questioning. The time is now and is already too late. But too late can become right on time—when the time is right. When the prophetic wild card is in play and a turning occurs, all that seems closed can open. Then mourning is remembered as the part of a process, too long and overdue, that can begin a reconciliation of enemies. The world begins anew.

Is it possible that a Genesis for the twenty-first century will be written in the language of modernity and with a Jewish inscription?

The most deeply engraved, the prophetic, long in exile, is alive.

Notes

1. AT THE CROSSROADS OF JEWISH IDENTITY

1. See Samuel Kaplan and Samuel Dresner, *Abraham Joshua Heschel: Prophetic Witness, 1907–1939*, 2 vols. (New Haven, CT: Yale University Press, 1998) and Edward Kaplan, *Spiritual Radical: Abraham Joshua Heschel, 1940–1972* (New Haven, CT: Yale University Press, 2008).

2. Richard Rubenstein, *After Auschwitz: Radical Theology and Contemporary Judaism* (Indianapolis: Bobbs-Merrill, 1966). See also Richard Rubenstein, *The Cunning of History: Mass Death and the American Future* (New York: Harper & Row, 1975).

3. Heschel's most extensive commentary on Israel is *Israel: Echo of Eternity* (New York: Farrar, Straus and Giroux, 1969).

4. Elie Wiesel's two-volume autobiography is *Wiesel, All Rivers Run to the Sea: Memoirs* (New York: Schocken, 1996) and *And the Sea Is Never Full* (New York: Schocken, 2000). For a critical assessment of Wiesel, see Mark Chmiel, *Elie Wiesel and the Politics of Moral Leadership* (Philadelphia: Temple University Press, 2001).

5. Irving Greenberg, "The Ethics of Jewish Power," in *Beyond Occupation: American Jewish, Christian, and Palestinian Voices for Peace*, ed. Rosemary Radford Ruether and Marc H. Ellis (Boston: Beacon Press, 1990), 22–74.

6. A seminal book of this emerging genre is Nathan Perlmutter and Ruth Ann Perlmutter, *The Real Anti-Semitism in America* (New York: Arbor House, 1982). After September 11, a number of books were written cataloging the "new" anti-Semitism; see, e.g.,

Phyllis Chesler, *The New Anti-Semitism: The Current Crisis and What We Must Do About It* (San Francisco: Jossey Bass, 2005).

7. Rubenstein develops this thought in *Cunning of History*, 70–71. In turn, Rubenstein cites the Holocaust historian Raul Hilberg, who authored one of the first histories of the Holocaust, now a classic. See Raul Hilberg, *The Destruction of the European Jews* (Chicago: Quadrangle Books, 1967). Like Rubenstein, Hilberg was a controversial historian. For his initial difficulties in publishing his groundbreaking book and the contested life that followed see his autobiography, *The Politics of Memory: A Journey of a Holocaust Historian* (Chicago: Ivan R. Dee, 1996).

8. See Edward Said, *Orientalism* (New York: Pantheon, 1978).

9. See William D. Miller, *A Harsh and Dreadful Love: Dorothy Day and the Catholic Worker Movement* (New York: Livewright, 1973) and his definitive biography, *Dorothy Day: A Biography* (San Francisco: Harper & Row, 1982). For my own stay at the Catholic Worker, see *A Year at the Catholic Worker* (New York: Paulist Press, 1978). Also see my biography of the co-founder of the Catholic Worker, *Peter Maurin: Prophet in the Twentieth Century* (New York: Paulist Press, 1980).

10. Marc H. Ellis, *Faithfulness in an Age of Holocaust* (Warwick, NY: Amity Press, 1986).

2. THE JEWISH QUEST FOR LIBERATION

1. Jane Hunter's work is cited in my *Toward a Jewish Theology of Liberation* (Maryknoll, NY: Orbis, 1987) and in the third edition of the same work (Waco: Baylor University Press, 2004), 172–74. For an early book on Israel's arms industry, see Aaron Klieman, *Israel's Global Reach: Arms Sales as Diplomacy* (London: Brassey's, 1985).

2. Emil Fackenheim, *God's Presence in History: Jewish Affirmations and Philosophical Reflections* (New York: New York University Press, 1970), 84.

3. *Toward a Jewish Theology of Liberation* has been published in three editions, the first in 1987 by Orbis Books. The second edition was published in 1989, also by Orbis, with a new final chapter and subtitle—*The Palestinian Uprising and the Future of the Jewish*

People. The updated and expanded third edition was published in 2004 by Baylor University Press with the subtitle *The Challenge of the 21st Century*. My discussion of New Jewish Agenda can be found in the first two editions. *Tikkun* is discussed in all three editions.

4. See James Cone, *Black Theology and Black Power* (New York: Seabury Press, 1969) and *A Black Theology of Liberation* (Philadelphia: J.P. Lippincott, 1970). They are currently available through Orbis Books. See also Gustavo Gutierrez, *A Theology of Liberation: History, Politics and Salvation* (Maryknoll, NY: Orbis, 1973). See also Gustavo Gutierrez, *On Job: God-Talk and the Suffering* (Maryknoll, NY: Orbis, 1987).

5. For Buber's writing on Palestine, Israel, and the Arabs, see *A Land of Two Peoples: Martin Buber on Jews and Arabs*, ed. Paul Mendes Flohr (New York: Oxford University Press, 1983).

6. Phillip Lopate, "Resistance to the Holocaust," *Tikkun* 4 (May–June 1989): 56.

7. Avishai Margalit, "The Kitsch of Israel," *New York Review of Books*, November 24, 1988, 23. I first came across this article as I was researching my sequel to *Toward a Jewish Theology of Liberation, Beyond Innocence and Redemption: Confronting the Holocaust and Israeli Power* (San Francisco: HarperSanFrancisco, 1990).

8. Ibid.

9. Ibid.

10. See Arthur Hertzberg's letter "An Open Letter to Elie Wiesel" in the *New York Review of Books*, August 18, 1988, 13–14. See also Hertzberg's compilation of early Zionist thinkers in *The Zionist Idea: A Historical Analysis and Reader* (Philadelphia: Jewish Publication Society of America, 1987).

11. For Judah Magnes, see *Dissenter in Zion: From the Writings of Judah L. Magnes*, ed. Arthur A. Goren (Cambridge, MA: Harvard University Press, 1982). See also Magnes's article "Toward Peace in Palestine," *Foreign Affairs*, January 1943, 239, 240–41. With regard to Hannah Arendt, see especially her writings on Zionism in Hannah Arendt, *The Jewish Writings*, ed. Jerome Kohn and Ron H. Feldman (New York: Schocken, 2007).

12. Hannah Arendt, "To Save the Jewish Homeland: There Is Still Time," in *The Jewish Writings*, 388–401.

13. Simha Flapan, *The Birth of Israel: Myths and Realities* (New York: Random House, 1987), 3–4.

14. Though Benny Morris has moved to the right politically, he remains committed to his historical unveiling of the birth of Israel. See his groundbreaking book *The Birth of the Palestinian Refugee Problem, 1947–1949* (Cambridge, UK: Cambridge University Press, 1988). For his most recent take on this time period, see Morris's *1948: A History of the First Arab-Israeli War* (New Haven, CT: Yale University Press, 2008). See also Ilan Pappe, *The Ethnic Cleansing of Palestine* (London: Oneworld, 2007).

15. Rafi Segal and Eyal Weizman, eds., *A Civilian Occupation: The Politics of Israeli Architecture* (London: Verso, 2003).

3. CAN JEWS REDEEM CHRISTIANITY?

1. See Irving Greenberg, "The Ethics of Jewish Power," in *Beyond Occupation: Jewish, Christian and Palestinian Voices for Peace*, ed. Rosemary Radford Ruether and Marc H. Ellis (Boston: Beacon Press, 1990) and Greenberg's earlier work on the different eras in Jewish history, "The Third Great Cycle of Jewish History," *Perspectives* (New York: National Jewish Resource Center, 1981).

2. For the witness people, see Stephen R. Haynes, *Reluctant Witnesses: Jews and the Christian Imagination* (Louisville: Westminster John Knox Press, 1995). For the most exhaustive theological work in this area, see Paul M. van Buren, *Discerning the Way: A Theology of the Jewish Christian Reality* (New York: Seabury, 1980) and *A Christian Theology of the People Israel, Part II* (New York: Seabury, 1983).

3. Often the books on the ecumenical dialogue were used as study guides for ecumenical commissions. For a very different and positive Jewish collaboration with Christians, in this case the Catholic Church during Vatican II, see Edward Kaplan, *Spiritual Radical*, 239–57.

4. Robert McAfee Brown, *Elie Wiesel: Messenger to All Humanity* (Notre Dame, IN: Notre Dame University Press, 1983). See also his primer on liberation theology, *Liberation Theology: An Introductory Guide* (Louisville: Westminster John Knox Press,

1993). For his own attempt to bridge the two, see Brown's "Christians in the West Must Confront the Middle East," in Ruether and Ellis, *Beyond Occupation*, 138–54.

5. Naim Ateek, *Justice and Only Justice: A Palestinian Theology of Liberation* (Maryknoll, NY: Orbis, 1989).

6. Desmond Tutu, "Apartheid in the Holy Land," Nuclear Age Peace Foundation, December 21, 2006, available at www.waging peace.org. See also an interview with Tutu regarding his cancellation in "Tutu Speaks," *City Pages*, November 21, 2007.

7. The Presbyterian resolution is found at www.pcusa.org/ga216. For reports on the 2006, 217th General Assembly's position with references to the initial 2004, 216th General Assembly's position, see Toby Richards Hill, "GA Overwhelmingly Approves Israel/Palestine Recommendation," at www.pcusa.org/ga217. At the same Web address, see "2004 GA's Israel/Palestine Language Replaced."

8. For the letter from Jewish organizations opposing divestment, see the Anti-Defamation League's Web site at www .adl.org/Interfaith/Letter-commissioners.asp.

4. MAPPING JEWISH DESTINY

1. My editorial was "Imagining Judaism and Jewish Life on the Threshold of the Twenty-first Century: A Commentary on the Wye Memorandum," *Journal of Church and State* 41 (Winter 1999): 5–12.

2. See Salmon H. Abu-Sitta, *Atlas of Palestine: 1948* (London: Palestine Land Society, 2004).

3. For a biography of Allon and a brief discussion of his plan, see Yigal Allon, *Native Son: A Biography* (Philadelphia: University of Pennsylvania Press, 2008).

4. Amos Kenan, "Four Decades of Blood Vengeance," *The Nation*, February 6, 1989, 155–56.

5. Yossi Sarid, "The Night of the Broken Clubs," *Ha'aretz*, May 4, 1989.

6. Gideon Spiro, "You Will Get Used to Being a Mengele," *Al Hasismar*, September 19, 1988.

7. Irving Greenberg's warning on triumphalism is found in his essay "Cloud of Smoke, Pillar of Fire: Judaism, Christianity and Modernity After the Holocaust," in *Auschwitz: Beginning of a New Era?*, ed. Eva Fleishner (New York: KTAV, 1977), 22.

8. On the burning children see ibid., 23.

9. Levinas develops this theme of Israel taking on the violence of the world in an essay written in the early 1950s and published under the title "Ethics and Spirit," in *A Difficult Freedom: Essays on Judaism*, trans. and ed. Sean Hand (Baltimore: Johns Hopkins University Press, 1990), 3–10. For an extended criticism of Levinas and politics, including the state of Israel, see Howard Caygill, *Levinas and the Political* (London: Routledge, 2002).

10. Jimmy Carter, *Palestine: Peace Not Apartheid* (New York: Simon & Schuster, 2006).

5. PROPHETS IN EXILE

1. Souad Dajani's e-mail, December 12, 2007, is a comment on Yuval Yoaz and Jack Khoury, "Civil Rights Group: Israel Has Reached New Heights of Racism," *Ha'aretz*, December 12, 2007.

2. I wrote this in response to Mr. Abdel Shafi's article "Two Hours Are Enough in Gaza," *This Week in Palestine*, December 2007.

3. Souad Dajani's e-mail of December 7, 2007, is a comment on Suzanne Goldenberg, "Waterboarding Greenlit at Top levels of Power," *The Guardian*, December 11, 2007.

4. Efraim Shmueli, *Seven Jewish Cultures: A Reinterpretation of Jewish History and Thought* (Cambridge, UK: Cambridge University Press, 1990).

5. Emmanuel Levinas, "Judaism and the Present," in *Difficult Freedom: Essays on Judaism*, trans. and ed. Sean Hand (Baltimore: Johns Hopkins University Press, 1990), 210.

6. Ibid., 208.

EPILOGUE: MOURNING FOR THE FUTURE

1. See James Wegg's April 25, 2007, review of *Kikes Like Me* at www.jamesweggreview.org.

2. Felicia Lee, "Vexing Questions of Jewish Identity," *New York Times*, December 17, 2007.

3. The London One State Group Declaration was issued in conjunction with the conference "Challenging the Boundaries: A Single State in Israel/Palestine." The conference was held at the Brunei Gallery at the University of London on November 17–18, 2007. The declaration and further materials can be found at www.onestate.net.